THE THIRD WORLD

THE THIRD WORLD

MIDDLE EAST

Author
HENRY BUCHER, Jr.

Editorial Director
DONALD K. SWEARER

Pendulum Press, Inc.
West Haven, Connecticut

This book was written in the 5732nd year of the Hebrew Era and 1,349 years after the flight (*Hegira*) of the Prophet Mohammad from Mecca to Medina. However, all dates in this book will conform to the calendar adopted by Western Christianity.

ISBN 0-88301-059-3 *Complete Set*
  0-88301-063-1 *This Volume*

Library of Congress Catalog Card Number 72-93316

Published by
Pendulum Press, Inc.
The Academic Building
Saw Mill Road
West Haven, Connecticut 06516

Printed in the United States of America

Cover Design by Ampersand Ltd.

CONTENTS

ABOUT THE AUTHOR

Henry Bucher, Jr. spent his childhood in China and the Philippines and completed his B.A. in history at the American University of Beirut, Lebanon, in 1958. He holds a masters in Theology from Princeton Seminary and a masters in history from the University of Wisconsin where he was a doctoral candidate at the time that he authored this book.

Mr. Bucher has lived and studied in Ghana and Gabon and has worked briefly in several countries including Israel where he helped construct homes for Jewish immigrants from Iraq in 1958.

FOREWORD

THE THIRD WORLD has been written to provide much needed materials on non-Western cultures. In the past, most studies of the non-Western world were chronological in organization or dealt with the regions studied by using the traditional themes of religion, politics, history, and so on. Very few, if any, offered the student a thematic perspective.

THE THIRD WORLD discusses the regions of Africa, East Asia, Latin America, Middle East, South Asia, and Southeast Asia from the perspective of societies and cultures in transition. This has been done in a variety of ways: by focusing on the problems of new nations struggling with the issues of economic development; by organizing the study around the major minorities of a region; by investigating the ways in which traditional norms and modern forms interact; and by seeing the problems of modern non-American cultures in the light of the anxieties, conflicts, and tensions of our own society.

In their own ways, the authors of each of the volumes have attempted to make their regions come alive. Each author teaches subjects related to the region about which he has written, and all have spent considerable time there. Consequently, they have a feel for the peoples and the cultures.

The authors of the volumes of THE THIRD WORLD are not only interested in these countries from an academic point of view. They also hope to be able to make a contribution to world understanding and world peace by increasing your knowledge of non-Western cultures, peoples, and societies.

THE THIRD WORLD has, in short, been written with a sense of urgency and a sense of mission. The urgency is the chaotic state of today's world. The mission is knowledge, not the kind of knowledge that comes from memorizing facts, but the understanding that comes from dispelling myths and from grappling with problems relevant to you and the world in which you live. You have a stake in the future of the world. It's a rapidly shrinking world in which the problems of the Third World are your problems. It's up to you to try to solve them. We hope that THE THIRD WORLD will be of some help along the way.

—Donald K. Swearer

INTRODUCTION

> *The most certain test by which we judge whether a country is really free is the amount of security enjoyed by minorities.*
>
> Lord Acton

To understand the Middle East is to discover our own origins, but it is much more. Today, more than ever before, the destinies of the world's peoples are interlocked economically, politically, and culturally. Whatever happens in tomorrow's world will be deeply influenced by the people who live today where Africa, Asia, and Europe have met, quarreled, borrowed, and traded since the beginning of civilization. To understand the Middle East is above all to know her people, to trace their footsteps over the centuries, and to try to see the world through their eyes both in the past and now.

Most books on the Middle East have separate chapters on history, culture, politics, and religion. Some treat each country individually. Still others describe the lives of famous leaders. We shall attempt another approach. The first chapter begins by describing the unchanging factors and recurring themes that have shaped and are still shaping the Middle East. These are then contrasted

1

with the changing factors which have to do with human development and migration. The remaining chapters focus on five specific peoples, bringing them briefly from their past into the modern world. Thus the themes of the first chapter will be embodied in their histories. We have chosen these five peoples as the focus of our study because: 1) their past role in history has been important; 2) they exist today in very different but significant forms, ready to play a unique role in the new Middle East; and 3) they represent some major geographical areas, cultures, and religions, often cutting across present national boundaries.

I have purposely chosen the Copts, Shias, Jews, Armenians, and Palestinians because they are minorities. The story of the Middle East is a story of many peoples, most of whom, no matter how great their past may have been, are today cultural or religious minorities. Minorities are often ignored in history books, or only mentioned in passing, a deficiency we recognize in our own textbooks in America. However, the story of a nation or a particular geographic area may be seen as an account of the interaction of its minorities with the majority population and with other minorities.

One aim of this book is to present the peoples of the Middle East to American students through themes that can easily be recognized as universal. With American minorities currently occupying headlines and challenging old myths and cherished conceptions of the majority, the careful student will be able to draw many striking parallels between the Middle East and America. He must be alert also for some startling contrasts.

Five minorities cannot adequately represent 150 million people in more than seventeen countries belonging to countless subdivisions of the three world religions that were born there. A further aim, therefore, of this book is to introduce the student to the immense complexity of the Middle East and to provide interpretative perspectives and bibliographical tools for further study. Each chapter has a brief annotated bibliography (in the back of this volume) combining some standard resources with recent ones. Biographies, art, novels, and poetry are also included focusing on people other than the minority under study. The general references will also be found at the end, including a list of available audio-visual materials, teaching guides, and organizations concerned with the Middle East.

Of all current issues in the Middle East, the most complex is the continuing struggle between Hebrew nationalism and Arab nationalisms. Therefore, we have included a brief chapter on the confrontation between Israel and the Palestinians. The student may be surprised by the long and strategic role America has played in this confrontation. No issue better illustrates our opening comment—that our past, our present, and our future are interlocked.

WHAT IS THE MIDDLE EAST?

Before people believed the Earth was round, terms like Orient for "the East" and Occident for "the West" were commonly used by Europeans who saw these areas only in geographical relation to themselves. Today "East" and "West" represent cultural divisions. In this book we are not using these terms in their Cold War sense. In fact we consider Russia to be Western, as are

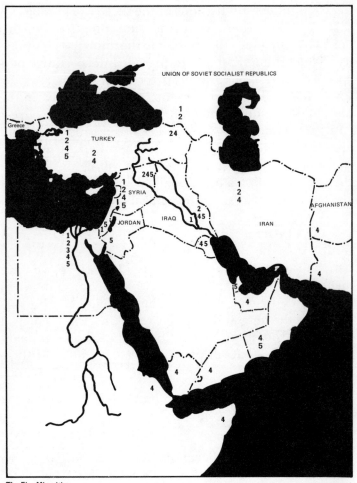

The Five Minorities

1 Jews

2 Armenians

3 Copts

4 Shias

5 Palestinians

Australia and the Republic of South Africa. Western here means the predominantly white, Christian-dominated areas of European origin.

Before 1900, Europeans spoke of China as the Far East. Almost every area from Vienna (Austria) to China was simply "the East." Around 1900, British naval officers began designating the area from Albania to Iran as the Near East. A United States Navy captain first used the term Middle East in 1902. In fact even today our attitudes may be influenced more than we realize by the military origins of our early contacts with the Middle East.

The French name for the Middle East, the "Levant" (referring to where the sun rises), also leaves us outside looking in. Is there no better name for this area than these of such obvious foreign origin? A fairer geographical term is Western Asia, but this excludes the very crucial nation of Egypt and her Arab neighbors in North Africa. What do Middle Easterners call themselves?

WHO ARE THE PEOPLE OF THE MIDDLE EAST?

Every geographical term has its obvious faults. We cannot define The Middle East without referring to its peoples. Some have tried to use cultural terms like the "Arab World." But this excludes modern Turkey, Iran, and the Western Jews, who began arriving after 1900. Others have suggested religious categories such as the "Islamic World." Even if we consider other Middle Eastern religions to be minorities, this term is far too inclusive. There are five hundred million Muslims in the world, and more than two-thirds live *outside* the area we call the Middle East. In fact, Pakistan and Indonesia together have more Muslims than the entire Middle East.

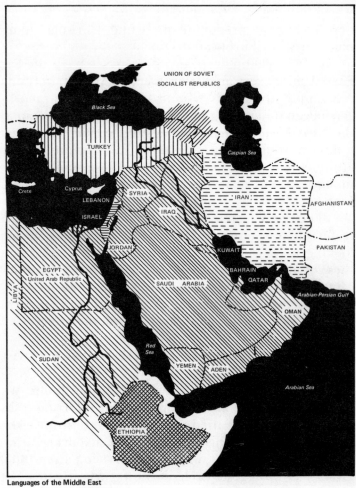

Languages of the Middle East

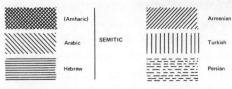

(Amharic)		Armenian
Arabic	SEMITIC	Turkish
Hebrew		Persian

Others have turned to the oldest and most common way of identifying peoples—by language. They call this area the Semitic Region, a term which not only covers the Arab countries and Israel of today, but also recalls their origins among the Semitic Akkadians, Canaanites, and Assyrians. Again, however, Turkish, Armenian, Kurdish, and Iranian (Persian) are not Semitic languages, while Amharic (Ethiopian) is.

There is no perfect term for the Middle East because we cannot force five thousand years and numerous peoples and nations under one adequate heading. Imagine for a moment what it would be like if, say, students in Turkey had to study Western Europe and North and South America in one course. Trying to name that course would give some idea of the problem involved here. Because there is no truly adequate term, we have chosen the most commonly used: Middle East. By the term Middle East, we mean Egypt, Libya and the Maghreb (Morocco, Algeria, Tunisia), Iran, Israel, Turkey, and the Arab states of Western Asia (Iraq, Jordan, Syria, Lebanon, Saudi Arabia, Yemen, Bahrein, Oman, Qatar, and the Arabic-speaking sheikdoms of the Arabian Peninsula). Bahrein, Oman, and Qatar were admitted to the United Nations as recently as October 1971. The name Syria when used alone refers to modern Syria. In the pre-World War I Ottoman Empire, Syria meant the central area of the fertile crescent between Egypt and Mesopotamia (Iraq), an area including also present-day Lebanon and Palestine. This we shall call Syria-Palestine.

It is helpful for clarity to spend so much time explaining our terms. But more than that, it has already told us much about the people of the Middle East, the complexities of the area, and our very Western way of approaching them.

I. THE MIDDLE EAST THROUGH HISTORY

PERMANENT FACTORS: Geography

Few factors have remained unchanged in the Middle East over the centuries—the nature of the land is one. The most obvious geographical feature in this region is large sections of arid lands bordered by fertile areas. Because rainfall is scarce, the irrigated areas are near rivers. Thus geography has made the verdant banks of the Nile and the lands near the Tigris and Euphrates Rivers the population centers of the past and present. Floods have brought periodic famine, especially in the valley of the less controllable Tigris and Euphrates.

Smaller rivers like the Jordan connect these two areas in what is called the "Fertile Crescent." While parts of the Egyptian, Arabian, and Syrian deserts are totally barren, some sections have always supported a small population of nomads who provided food and other aid for the important trade caravans of the past. Camels and horses have been largely replaced, however, by cars and planes. The discovery of oil in the twentieth century has revolutionized trade and politics and has brought tremendous social change in the area.

The low plain from the Arabian-Persian Gulf to the Mediterranean Sea (800 miles in length) is interrupted

Wide World Photo

Shown above is a view of Israel, Jordan, Syria, and Lebanon as seen from space on the Apollo VII flight.

by the mountains of Lebanon, rising in Sinai and embraced finally by the lofty mountains of Armenia. This range, particularly in Lebanon, has traditionally been the place where the influence from Westerners (Philistine, Greek, Roman, Crusader, and others) was met and resisted by the local inhabitants. From Syria extends the great rift that forms the Jordan Valley and the Dead Sea, and it continues as a geographical divide into East Africa.

The Taurus and Pontic Mountains of Turkey and the Elburz Mountains of Iran are part of a global range extending from the Pyrenees in Spain to the Himalayas in Asia. They divide the Middle East from Southern Europe.

Of the five seas surrounding the Middle East, the three greatest have always served as trade routes between Asia, Africa, and Europe. The northern tip of the Red Sea is only 80 miles from Port Said on the Mediterranean, and the Suez Canal that bridges this isthmus is only a century old. The two oldest trade routes from Asia and East Africa to Europe link the Red Sea and the Arabian Sea (through the Arabian-Persian Gulf) to the Mediterranean. It is no wonder that this area has always been a crossroads for trade, ideas, and conquest.

Some geographical factors encouraged people to live in isolation, developing local ideas and customs. This was true especially of the more mountainous regions of Lebanon and Turkey. An opposite role was played by the river valleys where boats and caravans spread ideas, trade, and population with relative ease. Natural resources were major influences in social and economic life. Lebanon and central Turkey, for instance, used their great forests to build empires having the best navy and maritime trade.

In general, the geographical factors which have influenced the Middle East for seven thousand years still operate today.

Recurrent Themes—Religion

Equally permanent, if less concretely visible, are certain themes which have shaped the people and history of the Middle East and are still at work in one form or another. The great drama of interaction of peoples has basic *motifs*, even though the characters and their civilizations change.

Some of these themes can be traced to geographical origins. Fertile lands are, of course, centers of civilization and trade. Where there are traders and the meeting of civilizations, there is a sharing of ideas. The Middle East has always been fertile in ideas, and for centuries these ideas were religious in nature. Religion in the West usually means a way of worship or a system of beliefs distinct from politics and the state. For the ancient and even some modern peoples of the Middle East, however, religion is a total way of living, encompassing every aspect of daily life and including such concepts as nation, law, and civilization. Even a man's name indicated his religion. Time was reckoned by religious events, as it is today, since the West has adopted one of the several religious calendars. There was no distinction between religion and politics: politics was an important way of expressing religion.

Three aspects of the religious theme occur repeatedly. First, in societies fortunate enough not to be threatened by outside powers, religion was often a most divisive element. Jews, Christians, Muslims, and other religious groups quarreled within their own ranks. Disagreement over religious interpretations were mixed

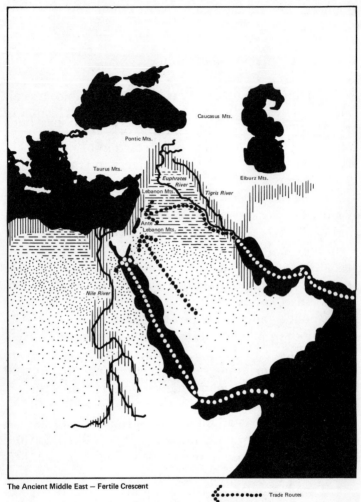

The Ancient Middle East — Fertile Crescent

with personality conflicts and competition between families. Nevertheless, when societies were confronted with some great task, like the Arab conquest of the seventh century, or threatened by outside forces, as were the Armenians and Jews in the twentieth century, religion became a powerful cement uniting the spiritual community. Sometimes all religions united to face a common invader. Thus, ironically, religion has been both a divisive and a unifying force in Middle Eastern history.

A second aspect of the religious theme is its dual nature. Religious zeal was very destructive to other religions and cultures. We would know more today about the pre-Christian Armenians if Gregory, who brought Christianity to Armenia, had not destroyed their "pagan" art and culture in the name of the new faith. On the other hand, the Coptic monks in Egypt and Jewish, Christian, and Muslim scholars during the "Golden Age" of Islam (900-1200 A.D.) preserved and helped develop each other's cultures. Thus, religion was both a destroyer and builder of civilizations.

Finally, one question emerges regularly within the religious theme. Who are the faithful and how are they recognized? This question can be asked in another way. Is a person a Jew, a Christian, or a Muslim because of his birth, or is faith something that can be adopted or accepted by a believer of any origin? In principle, most religions are open to whoever believes their doctrines, but in practice many faiths give special recognition to people who are related to a unique religious figure or to a family that has attained prestige over several generations. This question is still a very live one in the Middle East today.

Popular Thruway

Our second recurring theme is related to geography. The Middle East and particularly Syria-Palestine have always been the hub and often the terminus of endless migrations and military conquests. We tend to think of military movements and migrations in the Middle East as events in antiquity; Abraham's move from Ur in the Chaldees to the Promised Land in Palestine is perhaps the best known. Indeed every conquest from Egyptian-Babylonian times through the Crusades and Napoleon's invasion of Egypt (soon after the American Revolution) is crucial to understanding the present. But it is the present itself that is most often neglected in studying the Middle East. To an Egyptian or Israeli today, military movement means the wars of 1948, 1956, 1967, and 1973, while outside military intervention might mean the landing of the United States Marines in Lebanon in 1958. To Palestinian and Zionist alike, a discussion of migration would inevitably focus on the continuing immigration of Jews from other parts of the world to Israel. Western intrusion in the last centuries has been a major factor in transforming the Middle East.

Trader vs. Farmer

The oldest motif in Middle Eastern history is the recurring struggle between the herdsman/trader and the cultivator or farmer. The herdsman raised his sheep, moving from one fertile spot to another, trading and living a nomad's life. The farmer was sedentary, staying in one place to tend his crops; his fate was linked to the weather and to his piece of land. One of the oldest written accounts of this traditional struggle is found in the fourth chapter of Genesis, in which Cain, the farmer, kills his brother Abel, the herdsman. The opposite, however, has been more common in Middle Eastern history: desert nomads have periodically emerged from the semi-arid areas to overwhelm the cultivators. The greatest of these Semitic invasions from the desert was the Arab conquest of the seventh century.

Syria-Palestine as a "Third World"

The nomads were able to overwhelm the rich agricultural lands because the two great population centers, the Nile and the Tigris-Euphrates valleys, weakened themselves by constantly vying for control of the area between them. Caught in this rivalry were many peoples of Syria-Palestine and eastern Turkey. To draw a modern parallel, the two largest powers, the United States and the Soviet Union, compete for allies in their attempt to corner world markets, prestige, and power. The remainder of the world's nations have formed a "third force" refusing to join either side permanently. In the same way, many groups living in Syria, Turkey, and the Arabian Peninsula have for thousands of years been a "Third World" in the struggle between Egypt and Mesopotamia. Sometimes the smaller nations profited by playing off one big power against the other; sometimes they were annexed by one or the other; sometimes they were conquered and mistreated. It was often better to be a province of one of the powers than to be accused and sometimes punished by both. If Syria-Palestine wanted to be neutral, Egypt and Mesopotamia each assumed that this was tantamount to siding with the other.

The big empires taxed their provinces heavily and sometimes carried the peoples off into slavery. The luxury of their capitals was achieved at the expense of conquered neighbors. In times of greatest stress, subjugated peoples would band together. If still too weak, they could seek help from a more distant power, though this, too, was a great risk. If the distant power lost, revenge might be ruthless. If the distant power won, it would often join the power game and become as merciless as its predecessor. But in spite of its inferior power position, Syria-Palestine made great intellectual and spiritual contributions to the ancient world, including the development of monotheism and the invention of the alphabet.

Common Past

Another recurring theme may have already suggested itself: the Middle East is a mosaic of peoples whose languages, cultures, and religions have intermingled over time and changed over centuries, and who share a common past. People are not like archeological finds that can be put on a museum shelf with an identification tag. Whatever their condition, whatever empire they are under, they marry, have families, migrate if necessary, and pass on ideas that always change a little in the process. Often it has been the conqueror whose culture has been absorbed by the conquered. Some religions and ideas are older than others, as some unearthed jars are older than others; but the ethnic origins of all people are lost sooner or later in the crucible of antiquity, hidden with the secrets of the origin of man.

Superior Weapons Technology

A final theme is not unique to the Middle East. While many empires fell prey to internal weakness, it has often been superior weapons that have made the difference in international rivalries. First chariots, then the proper use of cavalry, then the introduction of firearms, and so on—each new stage allowed successive invaders to use better weapons to their advantage against superior numbers and traditional concepts of military codes. For example, when the Ottomans first used firearms against Mamluk Egypt, in the early 1500s, the Mamluks reacted in disgust. How, they asked, could the Ottoman Turks be true fighting men when they used a weapon with which a mere woman could singlehandedly kill several men? Not until firearms were adapted to horseback were they fully accepted in the Middle East.

CHANGING FACTORS: The Third World and the Middle Eastern Empires

By putting our permanent themes into flesh and bone we may begin to understand the changing factors in the Middle East. Rather than dwell on military details and the rise and fall of this or that empire, let us look at the rivalry in the ancient world between the two power centers which had tremendous impact on the Syrian-Palestinian "Third World."

Egypt's competition with the first Semites (Akkadians) starts around 3000 B.C., but here we will begin our story around 2000 B.C. with Egypt in active competition with Babylonia which controlled the Tigris-Euphrates valley. Babylonia proved less of a threat to Egypt than her successor, Assyria, who not only conquered Palestine by the seventh century B.C. but subdued Egypt herself as far south as Thebes. Although Assyria had to quell frequent outbreaks throughout her extended empire, it was a revolt at home, with help from the Medes and Babylonians, that destroyed Nineveh, her capital, in 612 B.C.

Although Babylon's empire was enlarged by Nebuchadnezzar, Egypt's next major rival in the Tigris-Euphrates valley was the Persian empire, which came into power when Cyrus the Great overthrew the Medes around 530 B.C. Persia conquered all of the Assyrian possessions plus all of what is Turkey today. Persia was the last of the great Eastern powers. While the rivalry between the Nile and the Tigris-Euphrates valleys continued into modern times, a new era was begun by invasions from the West.

The Third World and The Western Empires

Much as the semi-arid deserts were the places from which nomadic herdsmen periodically emerged from the East to conquer the farming peoples of the fertile river valleys, so the Mediterranean and the land route through today's Istanbul played the same role for Western conquerors. Western armies and navies prepared at their leisure for conquest, then attacked suddenly, often with new weapons, seizing the coastal areas.

Most conquests from the West were brief and hardly penetrated farther inland than the mountains of Lebanon. But in the fourth century B.C. a young Macedonian named Alexander swept back the Persian Empire and carved out the largest empire then known. Alexander the Great died in 323 B.C., only eleven years after he began his conquests. Within that decade, however, the boundaries of his empire became almost identical to what had been the domains of Persia for two hundred years. Alexander permanently introduced Greek culture into the Middle East. For the first time a Western language

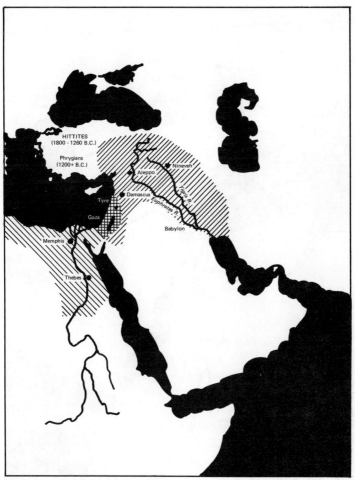

The Empires and the Third World (1300 - 650 B.C.)

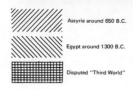

Assyria around 650 B.C.

Egypt around 1300 B.C.

Disputed "Third World"

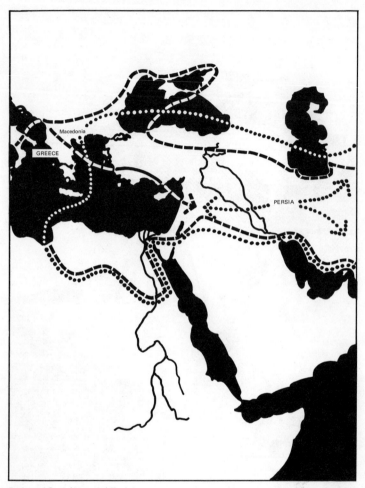

Persian and Greek (Alexander) Empires

Persian Empire
at 480 B.C.

Alexander's Empire
at 323 B.C.

became the dominant tongue. Nothing equaled the impact of Alexander until the Islamic conquest one thousand years later.

From the West, Roman conquest followed the Greek in the first century B.C.—about the same time that Persia's power was restored under the Parthians. The Romans called their campaign the pacification of Syria, which meant military domination for political and commercial reasons. Although the Nile valley was now the "breadbasket" for the Roman Empire rather than a center of power, peoples living between the Roman and the new Persian power were still very much a third world. Rome had to deal not only with Jewish rebellions in Palestine but also with the spread of a religion begun by a handful of Jews who claimed that a local carpenter and teacher, Jesus of Nazareth, was the long-awaited Messiah. At first the followers of Jesus came mostly from the poorer classes, but by 312 A.D. even the Roman emperor, Constantine, adopted Christianity, renaming Byzantium, the capital of the Eastern Roman Empire, Constantinople. Even though Rome itself fell to "barbarians" in 476 A.D., this so-called Byzantine Empire remained the champion of Greek culture and Christianity until the rise of Islam two hundred years later.

The last of the great Semitic invasions from the desert pushed back the Byzantine Empire but could not take Constantinople. This Islamic conquest under the Arabs moved eastward across Persia and pushed westward across North Africa into Spain and southern France, but was halted at Tours in 732. Under Islam, science, medicine, philosophy, and art flourished. Baghdad became a world capital of learning between the tenth and twelfth centuries.

In the eleventh century a new conquering people emerged, the Seljuk Turks. Related to the Mongols, these Turks from central Asia became Muslims and took over the leadership of Islam from the Arabs and Persians, introducing a new religious fervor and militancy. The Arabs had allowed people of all faiths to make pilgrimages to Jerusalem, but the Turks reversed this policy. Europe was disturbed enough by this threat to Christendom to launch the first Crusade (1097) in hopes of capturing the Holy Land from Islam.

The Crusaders pushed their way into Syria-Palestine and set up coastal states which resisted the many Muslim attempts to overthrow them. But the Islamic world was weakened by rivalry between the Ottoman Turks, who took over from the Seljuks and the powerful Mamluks of Egypt. The Mamluks were Muslims, former slave-soldiers, who had not only seized control of Egypt but had also taken over Syria-Palestine. The Mongol invasions from the East threatened both the Ottomans and the Mamluks. Once again the third world of Syria-Palestine was sandwiched between Egypt (Mamluks) and Mesopotamia (Mongols) with the Crusaders from the West a third invading force. As usual, the decisive battle was fought on Syrian-Palestinian soil. The defeat of the Mongols at Goliath Springs in Palestine by the Mamluks in 1260 and the Mamluk defeat of the Crusaders thirty years later preserved the dominance of Islam in the Middle East in the same way that the Battle of Tours (732) in France assured the dominance of Christianity in Europe.

With firearms from Europe, the Ottoman Turks conquered Mamluk Egypt and renewed the Islamic ad-

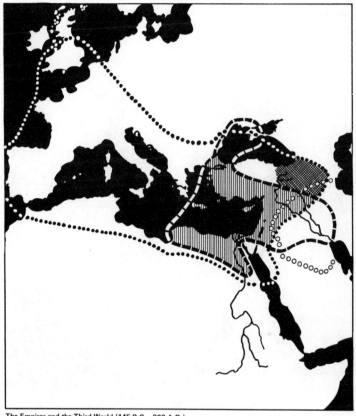

The Empires and the Third World (145 B.C. - 360 A.D.)

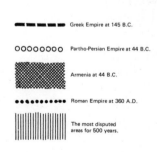

Greek Empire at 145 B.C.

Partho-Persian Empire at 44 B.C.

Armenia at 44 B.C.

Roman Empire at 360 A.D.

The most disputed
areas for 500 years.

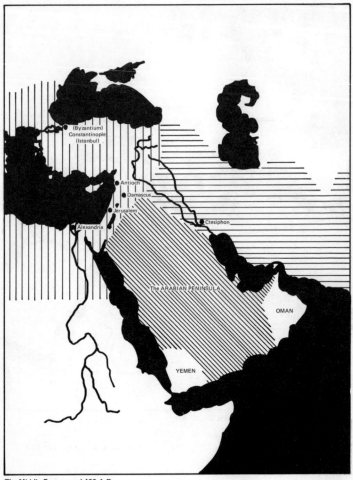

The Middle East around 400 A.D.

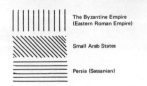

The Byzantine Empire
(Eastern Roman Empire)

Small Arab States

Persia (Sassanian)

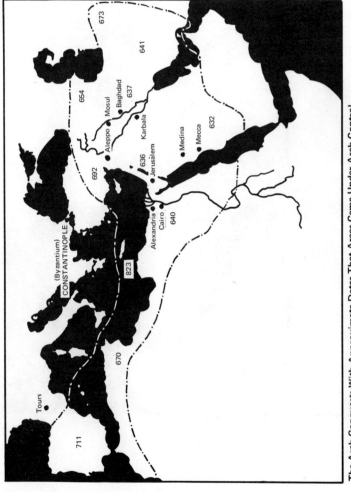

The Arab Conquests With Approximate Dates That Areas Came Under Arab Control

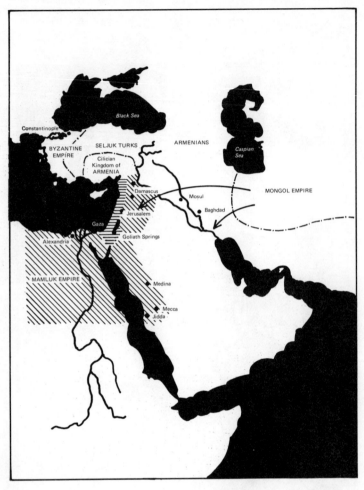

Crusader States 1150 - 1187

Mamluk Empire around 1341

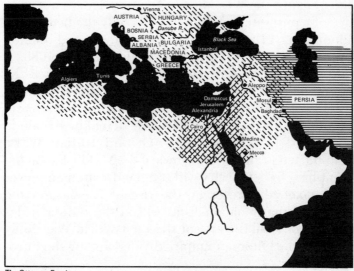

The Ottoman Empire

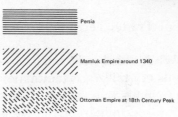

Persia

Mamluk Empire around 1340

Ottoman Empire at 18th Century Peak

vance against the West with even more vigor. Their capture of Constantinople in 1453 was only the beginning. Conquering Hungary, the Turks threatened Vienna several times, their last defeat being as late as 1683. A little more than a century later Napoleon invaded the Ottoman Empire in what he called a scientific expedition into Egypt. But Napoleon also had political and military reasons for his expedition. France's defeat by Britain in India and in America (French and Indian Wars, 1756-63) led France to look toward the Middle East as the next phase in her rivalry with England. Ottoman power was weakened further by the rise of Russia and the growth of many nationalisms within the Ottoman domains. Not until the end of the First World War, however, was the Ottoman Empire divided among the European powers.

Rise of Trade, Technology, And New Ideas

While this brief sketch of centuries of history may help us crystallize certain major events, it is difficult to span so many years in so few pages. Once more our facts and figures, military in nature, tell us that men met and struggled in significant encounters. Yet the exchange of ideas particularly in modern times between the West and the Middle East has been far more responsible for the great changes that have taken place than hundreds of years of military incursions.

This exchange of ideas did not begin with contacts with the West, for every conquest in the Middle East brought new concepts that, like the conquering people themselves, were gradually assimilated. However, for three reasons modern contacts with the West are different: (1) world trade increased rapidly in importance after

European discoveries in the New World during the fifteenth century; (2) after the Industrial Revolution in Europe, Western technology was injected into Middle Eastern society; and (3) technology combined with nineteenth century European political ideas to form a revolution in government and social life. Sometimes all three factors were at work simultaneously, but we shall separate them for discussion.

World Trade

Trade has always been important within the Middle East, and we have already mentioned that two routes between West and East crossed there. Even the Crusaders' influence in the Middle East was more economic than religious. Long after their religious zeal had worn off, Crusaders who remained turned their coastal castles into fortified trading posts. As middlemen between Europe (Venice and Genoa) and the Middle East, they made excellent profits. Just before the Crusader Kingdoms were destroyed by the Mamluks, Marco Polo traveled from Venice to China (1271), the first European to report extensively on this international trade route.

It is believed by some that Columbus in his search for Eastern riches in 1492 hoped to amass enough gold to pay for a crusade big enough to conquer the Holy Land permanently. But his discovery of America affected the Middle East in a very different way. Shortly thereafter, Vasco da Gama discovered a way around Africa to the riches of the East (1497-99). In the Middle East, the Ottoman Turks were bringing the entire Fertile Crescent under their influence and were threatening Vienna. Portugal and the Ottomans were the only two great maritime powers in the late fifteenth and early sixteenth centuries.

Portugal was dominant on the seas because of her use of cannons and newer methods of sailing, borrowed primarily from Arab technology. For nations lacking sea control to the Far East, the Middle East became more strategic than ever. Furthermore, European merchants were able to negotiate special commercial treaties with Istanbul, lowering their duties on imports and exports. In spite of the new sea route to the East, trade with the West continued to flourish by the land route through the Middle East.

When France, England, and Egypt built the Suez Canal in 1869 the Middle East became critical for sea trade. Every major power in Europe was interested in the Middle East for economic as well as strategic reasons. Germany and Britain competed for rights to link Baghdad to the West by rail, in hopes of bypassing Suez. To the north of the Ottoman Empire, Czarist Russia was on the rise. During the winter months her northern ports were frozen. The only way for her naval and trading vessles to operate freely was through possession of ports in the Black Sea. Russia's desire to control the Dardanelles, where Istanbul guarded the entrance to the Mediterranean, was to play an important role in the future of the Middle East.

In the twentieth century, oil became the most important resource in the Middle East. Today, 60 percent of the non-Communist world's crude oil reserves are in the Middle East—mostly in Iran, Saudi Arabia, and Kuwait. The Middle East supplies half of the oil used by Britain and Western Europe and over 80 percent of Japan's oil. The Middle East accounts for over one-fourth of the world's annual oil production. Oil from the Middle East is in great demand because a barrel of oil costs six cents to produce in Kuwait, around twenty cents in Iran and

Saudi Arabia, in comparison to fifty-one cents in Venezuela, eighty-two cents in Indonesia, and $1.75 in the United States.

Rise of Technology

Although Europe lagged behind the Middle East in science during the Middle Ages, the opposite became true after 1500. The invention of printing facilitated the spread of European ideas to the Middle East by 1600, but the most direct impact of the West on the Middle East was not felt until after the Industrial Revolution around 1750. When the steam engine was invented, the economic, military, and social life of Europe changed completely. The search for new markets, quests for empires to protect these markets, an evangelical awakening with emphasis on foreign missions—all these were behind a vital new burst of energy that propelled the West onto the doorstep of the Middle East.

The Suez Canal was only the first and most striking contribution of European technology to the Middle East. Technology continued to be used to further both the trade and political goals of the European powers.

Rise of New Ideas

The Ottomans are said to have been to the Arabs what the Romans were to the Greeks. As Roman law and organization spread Greek philosophy and wisdom, so the Ottoman empire united Islam and Arab philosophy and for four hundred years spread it across the Middle East. The Sultan, who lived in Istanbul (formerly Constantinople), was the "shadow of God on earth." His strength was dependent not only on Islam as a religion,

Built in 1869, the Suez Canal was the sight of a bitter struggle in 1956. Britain, France, and Israel invaded the canal zone, but pressure from the United States and the Soviet Union forced them to withdraw.

but also on Islamic law, recognized throughout the empire. Furthermore, he was the supreme commander of a very efficient military system.

Under Islamic law, the Christians and Jews were the most favored among the empire's minorities. Judaism had given birth to Christianity and Islam had been greatly influenced by both. The Koran states: (II:62)

> Lo! those who believe (in that which is revealed unto thee, Muhammad), and those who are Jews and Christians . . . —whoever believeth in Allah on the last day and doeth right—surely their reward is with their Lord, and no fear shall come upon them, neither shall they grieve.

While Jews and Christians regarded others as non-Jews and non-Christians, the Muslim Arabs followed this Koranic advice and recognized Jews and Christians as "protected people." This privileged position of Jews and Christians was most evident during the "golden age" of Islam (900-1200), as we shall see in Chapters II, III, and IV.

During Ottoman control of the Middle East (1450-1917), this same Islamic concept was incorporated into their government and expanded to include other minorities. The Ottomans let religious and ethnic minority groups rule themselves indirectly. Orthodox Christians were one "nationality," or *millet* in Turkish. They lived in their own quarters in the big cities or in their own villages under their own leadership, represented in the Ottoman government by their Patriarch in Istanbul. The Jews were also a *millet* as were the Armenians. Sizable minorities were simply recognized by the Sultan as other *millets*. The head of each *millet* was a member of the

Ottoman government in Istanbul, but each *millet* was an isolated, self-sufficient unit living its own life, not unlike the Amish, for example, in America today. The *millets* paid more taxes than the orthodox Muslim majority population, but their people could not be drafted into the military and often they were not allowed to bear arms. Thus the Ottoman system was tolerant of minorities; however, it made special demands in return. But this system encouraged divisions, gave more power to the clergy, and increased internal religious rivalries.

Within these general statements we must remember that one Sultan was quite different from another. Peace for minorities sometimes depended on who was in power. In troubled times, Christians or Jews could move to the comparative safety of the larger cities like Cairo, Alexandria, Damascus, Aleppo, or Baghdad. Or they could settle in the mountainous areas of Lebanon as sects had always done for self-protection. They could also become assimilated—that is, become Muslims, which was often the easiest and most profitable solution.

One other solution was open to the minorities—it, too, had been used for centuries. This was to seek outside support or protection from a sizable Western power. Such a solution could be very profitable, but it carried high risks. If the outside power was big enough and gave its full support, the minority group was treated well. But if the political winds shifted, the group was almost always viewed as traitorous.

Ottoman possessions in North Africa were the first to fall under European power with little resistance from Istanbul. The Arab countries along Africa's northern coast had never been under firm Ottoman control, which made European domination easier. France occupied Algeria in 1830 and seized Tunisia in

1882. A year later Britain began her occupation of Egypt, ostensibly to collect debts incurred by Egypt during the building of the Suez Canal. In 1907, France assumed responsibility for protecting Morocco, never a part of the Ottoman Empire. Four years later Italy annexed Libya. North Africa had become part of three European colonial empires.

As the Ottoman Empire continued to decline, the West increased its contacts with the minorities under the Ottomans. In some cases the *millets* asked the European powers to be their spokesmen to the Sultan in Istanbul; at other times the Europeans used the minorities as an entrance into Ottoman politics. In either case this policy was officially called Western "protection" of minorities. Some minorities, however, felt safer protected by Muslims than being protected by the West from Islam.

France began this system of protection as early as the 1500s, extending her aid to the Maronites of Lebanon. The Maronites were Eastern Christians who had sought close ties with the Roman Catholics as a result of contacts made three centuries earlier during the crusades. Czarist Russia followed France in the late 1700s, protecting the Eastern Orthodox Christians; later she also protected the Armenians (Chapter V). Britain watched over the Jewish *millet* and the non-orthodox Christian groups. Many of the quarrels that brought European powers into direct conflict with the Ottomans involved disputes among various minorities over Holy Places. Because Jerusalem was holy to the three major faiths, it was considered a special zone in the Ottoman Empire, a zone responsible directly to Istanbul.

These direct conflicts were often less significant than other ways in which European protection found expression—such as the opening of schools. Western schools, usually founded by missionaries, introduced new ideas, many of which stemmed from the American and French revolutions. Unsuccessful in converting significant numbers of Muslims to Christianity, the missions often brought Eastern Christians into Western denominations, creating even more religious factions in the cradle of Christianity.

Since the mission schools taught European languages and ideas, their students were quickly employed by Western business enterprises. Many, the younger generation particularly, began imitating the West as a sign of advancement. They moved to the commercial centers, creating over a period of time a new social class—the modern city merchants. Unlike the merchants of the past, their loyalty to their *millet* and village life was replaced by an undefined allegiance to the European government they served and imitated.

But this was only part of the social revolution that resulted from new ideas. The Western schools had brought a form of "unconscious integration." When children of Armenians, Greeks, Jews, Copts, Druzes, and other ethnic-religious groups came to one school from their own closed communities, they began to learn about each other directly rather than depending on their parents' and grandparents' concepts of other people. The *millets* were thus being opened up to the changing world around them.

As might be expected, the Ottoman rulers were not happy about these changes. As the minorities' economic and social position in the empire was elevated, the majority population inevitably became suspicious. In fact the minorities were accused, during the last part of the 1800s and the beginning of the 1900s, of being increasingly dangerous to the greater Islamic community and disloyal to the Ottoman Empire. But some minorities refused to be Westernized, as they had resisted being "Islamized" for centuries. They saw their role as a special one in the new Middle East. The Copts of Egypt are a good example of this position, as we shall see in Chapter II. Other groups, like the Jews and the Armenians, became identified with those of the same origin in other parts of the world.

A few Muslims thought of abandoning their religion and accepting Western ideas in order to build a modern Middle East. Others suggested that Islam should be modernized to compete with the West. But there were also those who wanted to unite Islam (Pan-Islamism) and resist the hated European intrusion.

World War I and Nationalism As A New Idea

About the time that the United States was recovering from her Civil War, nationalism was on the rise in the Middle East. Nationalist feelings were built around language groups (Arabic, Armenian, Kurdish, etc.) and were directed against the Sultan's regime in Istanbul. In 1908, a group of young Turks who wanted a democracy with a constitution achieved their goal, with the aid of a number of these nationalists. The latter hoped thus to achieve autonomy for their groups.

But the Turkish Revolution of 1908, although it was the first modern social revolution in the Middle East, did not fulfill the hopes of the minorities in the Ottoman Empire. On the contrary, it attempted to force all groups to become part of a centralized, powerful Turkish state. Minorities had less freedom than they had enjoyed

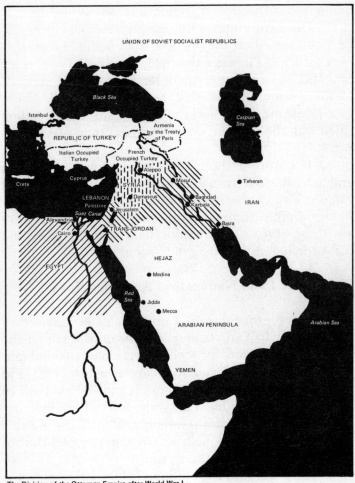

UNION OF SOVIET SOCIALIST REPUBLICS

Black Sea

Istanbul

Armenia
by the Treaty
of Paris

Caspian Sea

REPUBLIC OF TURKEY

Italian Occupied
Turkey

French
Occupied Turkey

Aleppo

Mosul

Teheran

Cyprus

Crete

SYRIA

Damascus

Baghdad

Karbala

IRAN

LEBANON

Palestine

Jerusalem

Suez Canal

Alexandria

TRANS-JORDAN

Basra

Cairo

HEJAZ

EGYPT

Medina

Red Sea

Jidda

Mecca

ARABIAN PENINSULA

Arabian Sea

YEMEN

The Division of the Ottoman Empire after World War I

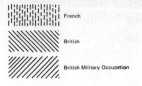

French

British

British Military Occupation

under the Sultaň. Many of them, now more nationalist than ever, sought more active help from European powers for complete release from Turkish control.

The alliance of Turkey with Germany and Austria in World War I offered an ideal opening for the minorities in the Middle East to side with France, Britain, and Russia against the Ottomans. In an effort to consolidate minority nationalisms against Turkey, the Allies followed up gifts of arms with promises that autonomous Arab states would be carved out of the Turkish Empire after the war. At this time, moreover, Britain let it be known that she favored a home in Palestine for the Jews. Assured of support from the rebellious minorities in the Middle East, the Allies made plans secretly among themselves which contradicted their agreements with the peoples of the Middle East.

At the Paris Peace Conference in 1919, President Woodrow Wilson's well-known Fourteen Points dominated the discussion. What most excited the majority of participants at the conference was the President's concept of "self-determination" for all people, an idea that the people of the Middle East interpreted as the independence they had been struggling for. However, the big powers' interpretation was that the Middle East should be divided up into "spheres of influence." These spheres correspond closely to the agreements made between France, Britain, and Russia during the war. Britain and France, by mandate from the League of Nations, were made responsible for specific areas until they were ready for total independence. The boundaries drawn in Paris and Lausanne (1919-23) are basically the political divisions in the Middle East today. Only Palestine was to undergo major changes in 1948.

The Communist Revolution in Russia in 1917 brought in leaders who made public the Allied secret treaties during World War I, and the Soviets refused to participate in the colonization of Turkey's former empire. Thus, although Islam could not accept communism's denial of religion, many Middle Eastern peoples looked at Communist Russia from the beginning in a favorable political light.

Ottoman Turkey emerged from World War I as the Turkish Republic under Mustafa Kemal (Ataturk). She was allowed to keep the areas that had a majority of Turks. Although defeated, Turkey remained independent while ironically the minorities who had helped the Allies defeat her remained under European control. To the frustrated minorities the situation was grossly unfair. World War I left them with the bitter feeling that they had been deceived by the West.

From World War I Until Today

But troubles were not the fault of outside forces alone. Between the two world wars, internal strife set the stage for modern Arab politics. The most important Arab competition was between the Hashemite dynasty of Mesopotamia and southern Syria, and the Saud family of the Southern Arabian Peninsula. The British believed they had solved Saudi-Hashemite territorial claims by presiding over the division of Southern Syria and Mesopotamia into Palestine, Trans-Jordan, and Iraq. Two Hashemite brothers, Abdullah and Feisal, were given the thrones of Trans-Jordan and Iraq respectively under British protection, while Ibn Saud was recognized as King of Saudi Arabia.

The present King Hussein of Jordan is the grandson of the former King Abdullah of Trans-Jordan. King Feisal II of Iraq was murdered in the revolution of 1958, in Baghdad. After 1958, only five monarchies in the major Middle Eastern nations remained: Iran, Jordan, Saudi Arabia, Morocco, and Libya. Libya's monarchy was overthrown in 1969. Her new Revolutionary Command Council is headed by a then twenty-seven-year-old Prime Minister.

Today the Hashemite kingdom of Jordan continues its family feud with Saudi Arabia. Both countries are regarded by surrounding Arab nations as monarchical museum pieces of European colonialism while the West tends to credit the four monarchies with stability—a stability undergirded by Western arms and direct intervention when necessary to secure the throne.

The Arab republics look to Egypt for leadership in the Arab World today. Various experiments in Arab unity have been tried. In 1958, Syria joined with Egypt in forming the United Arab Republic, a name that Egypt kept after Syria withdrew in 1961. In 1971, Libya, Syria, and Egypt joined in the Federation of Arab Republics, the latest, largest, and boldest attempt in regional cooperation in the Arab Middle East since the Ottoman Empire.

Whatever their internal differences, most of the Arab leaders were united by the gradual creation of a Jewish state in Palestine between the world wars. The British began to carry out the policy that one of their Cabinet members, Lord Balfour, had outlined in 1917, to win Jewish support for the war effort. The Balfour declaration began by saying that "His Majesty's Government views with favour the establishment in Palestine of a national home for the Jewish people. . . ." There was little dispute over the first part of this very short document, but its close created real problems: ". . . . it being clearly understood that nothing shall be done which may prejudice the civil and religious rights of existing non-Jewish communities in Palestine, or the rights and political status enjoyed by Jews in any other country."

As we shall see in our chapters dealing with Jews and Palestinians, British attempts to do justice to all parties in Palestine proved impossible. The division of Palestine in 1948 is at the bottom of the most crucial issue facing the Middle East today (see Chapter VII).

A fundamental cause of the transformation of the modern Middle East, then, was the rapid introduction of new ideas, the most important of which was nationalism. Nationalism, which took many forms, looked primarily to the past as a foundation for the building of new hopes and dreams. As we look at five different peoples—how each saw its past and how each envisions the present and future—we will see the basic themes discussed in this chapter emerge time and again in different historical circumstances.

Since our main purpose is to understand the people of the Middle East by looking at five minorities, the historical sketch in this chapter is purposely brief. Each following chapter will fill in relevant historical events. The story of the Copts will tell us about the emergence of Egypt as a modern nation. Shias cannot be described without reference to Iraq, Iran, and even India and Pakistan. The history of the Jews involves world history but focuses on Israel after 1948. Armenia's story is closely related to the last days of the Ottoman Empire, while the Palestinian people are at the heart of the present conflict between Israel and her neighbors.

QUESTIONS FOR DISCUSSION

1. What basic recurrent themes in Middle Eastern history seem to you to be true also of Western (especially American) history?

2. Many Western ideas about Islam, Arabs, Turks, and Middle Eastern life came from Crusader reports. What kinds of biases would Crusaders most likely have? What aspects of Middle Eastern life would they know best from their castles on the coast? About what aspects would they be most ignorant?

3. Why is the Middle East considered a part of the "Third World" today? Do you think competition for control of the Middle East by the big powers is greater today than in the past? Why?

II. THE COPTS: THE ORIGINAL EGYPTIANS

*Those who live in Egypt have a different understanding of
the desert from those who live in Europe or America. In
some places . . . the desert has become the testing ground for
nuclear energy and a variety of means of destruction. . . .
Here in Egypt the desert has provided a testing ground for
the souls of men.*

Professor Otto Meinardus, Cairo

ORIGINS

The Middle East has been called a "museum of religious and linguistic history." The origin and growth of
the Copts in the Nile Valley show the truth of this state-
ment. The present Coptic language is the latest stage in a
long evolutionary process beginning with the language
of the Pharaohs and influenced by many conquering
tongues, such as Greek, brought to the Nile Valley
twenty-three hundred years ago by Alexander the Great.

The Copts are a mixture of the oldest known inhabitants of the Middle East with every successive conqueror. Today they number four million in what is now
the Arab Republic of Egypt, a country of almost forty
million. The word *Egypt* itself comes from "Copt," the

Greek way of saying *Ha-ka-Ptah*, or "the land where the God Ptah is worshipped." Coptic continued as a language and a nationality when Egypt became the breadbasket of the Roman Empire.

ARRIVAL OF CHRISTIANITY

Christianity was first brought to Egypt under Roman rule. Tradition says that Saint Mark introduced this new Jewish sect around 37 A.D., first to Jews in Alexandria. Within a decade the Jewish Christian leaders in Jerusalem decided that bonds of faith were more important than family ties of blood and kinship. They decided that converts to Christianity should be sought not only from among Jews but also from among those who worshipped other deities. Anyone who believed that Christ was the promised Messiah could become Christian. In spite of persecution, or perhaps because of it, the faith spread. Some of the persecuted escaped into the desert to live a secluded life. Others chose to be monks for spiritual reasons. The best known Coptic monk is Saint Anthony (270 A.D.). Partly by force of circumstances, then, monasticism began in Egypt and is still a tradition among some Copts. It is today held in highest regard as the ideal life; leaders of the Coptic Church are chosen from desert monks. Coptic art, produced in secluded monasteries, was uniquely Egyptian, comparatively unaffected by sophisticated cosmopolitan centers like Alexandria. Furthermore, these artists used commonplace materials like wood, cloth (linen and wool), and limestone rather than granite, gold, and silk. This art was the expression of Coptic life and faith along the Nile.

By 313 A.D., when Constantine embraced Christianity in the name of the whole Roman Empire, the majority of Egyptians were Christian by faith and Coptic by nationality. The Copts had helped Christianity spread to the Sudan and Ethiopia. But the end of persecution allowed Christians of the Roman world the luxury of disagreeing over theological doctrines. Often these disagreements had political overtones, and serious attempts to come to agreement were seldom successful. Christian doctrines were hotly debated at the ecumenical Councils of Nicea (325 A.D.), Ephesus (431 A.D.), and Chalcedon (451 A.D.). The Copts disagreed with the official Byzantine position at these councils. The religious question concerned the nature of Christ, whether He was divine or human; the political problem was simply that Egyptian nationalism was in conflict with Byzantine (Graeco-Roman) nationalism.

ENTRY OF ISLAM

The Copts were so persecuted by their fellow Byzantine Christians for their refusal to accept the dual nature of Christ as defined at Chalcedon, that the Arabs, when they conquered Egypt around 650, were actually welcomed by most of the Copts. Other minorities, including Jews, eagerly anticipated the Arabs for similar reasons. Their hopes had some basis. The Prophet Mohammed had forbidden the persecution of Jews and Christians, but Islam required them to pay a sizable tax. In return their property and lives were protected. The minorities were also forbidden to bear arms. While they may not have had an ideal life under Muslim rule, they were happier than they had been under Christian domination for three hundred years.

Many Copts became Muslims after the Arab conquest; some converted because they liked Islam, some sought material gain, still others reacted to heavy social pressure by assimilating. Those who remained Christian soon became a minority. Since that time, the word *Copt* has signified a religion more than a nationality. The Copts rapidly adopted Arabic, and the ancient Coptic language was used only in their religious liturgy.

RELATIONS WITH THE WEST

The Copts are loyal to family, to tradition, and to their religion. They have also remained remarkably loyal to Egypt. In spite of this fidelity, their faith linked them to the Christian West and made them suspect in times of crisis. After the great soldier Saladin stopped the Crusaders (Richard the Lionhearted among them), he ruled in Egypt until his death. It is not surprising that after his bitter experience with the Christian Crusaders Saladin was particularly hard on the Copts. But only on rare occasions have Copts led revolts. In times of serious crisis the Copts asked the Roman Catholic Pope in Rome to act in their behalf. But since the Coptic Church did not recognize the Pope as its supreme pontiff, Rome was usually unwilling to intervene. Some Copts, however, subsequently recognized Rome and formed the Coptic Catholic Church.

Minorities had their own sections in the bigger cities of the Middle East. But the Coptic and Jewish quarters were not like the later ghettos of Europe. On the contrary, they were comparable to American suburbs. The Copts, Jews, and other minorities were successful traders and craftsmen. The Copts were traditionally in charge of the official Egyptian treasury. It is interesting that they were trusted with the nation's money even though they were not allowed to bear arms. The Copts were also responsible for tax collecting, an important but difficult task. Certainly a resentment was felt by the Muslim majority toward Jewish and Christian minorities, who were economically more successful that the Muslim majority was. For years, Jews and Christians were restricted from riding horseback and had to wear distinctive turbans, belts, and shoes. Sometimes these restrictions were relaxed by one ruler only to be reinstituted by his successor.

With the coming of Western ideas during the Ottoman period, the minorities in the cities formed a merchant class which tended to imitate the West. In Egypt this was more true of the Syrian Christians, Armenians, and Jews than of the Copts, who emphasized their "Egyptianness."

In 1798, when Napoleon Bonaparte invaded Egypt with thirty-seven thousand soldiers, the Copts were at their lowest point numerically and economically. Three years of French occupation made things worse for them because other Egyptians suspected that they were responsible for this latest European incursion. Napoleon's declaration that he had become a Muslim was seen as a ploy to win the support of the majority. When Napoleon landed in Alexandria, a suggestion was made by some Muslims to exterminate all the Copts in Cairo; fortunately it was not carried out. Napoleon kept the Copts in their traditional position with the treasury and organized a Coptic military legion.

COPTS AND EGYPT

When the Ottoman Turks regained control of Egypt from the French, many Copts suffered because they had cooperated with Napoleon. The usual high and low periods for minorities continued through the 1800s leaving them to the whim and wisdom of those in power. Under Mohammed Ali (1805-49), Egypt and Syria-Palestine were almost autonomous, with loose ties to the Sultan in Constantinople. Minorities rose to high positions under Mohammed Ali's long rule—he was a Turkish-speaking Albanian himself. His preference was for Armenians, partly because they spoke Turkish.

When one Pasha (Prime Minister) decreed in 1854 that all Egyptians regardless of religion could bear arms and should be eligible for the military draft, the Copts first welcomed this as an end to discriminatory legislation. Life in the military, however, quickly forced many to reconsider the value of this privilege.

A new enthusiasm invigorated the Copts during the middle of the nineteenth century. New Coptic high schools had been founded which taught technical skills necessary for building a modern Egypt. In addition to Arabic, Coptic, Turkish, French, Italian, English, and religion, students now had to study science and mathematics. Muslims also had schools, as did other ethnic and religious groups, but these had been founded to preserve and spread traditional religious concepts and values. The oldest and most famous such school in Egypt is the one thousand-year-old mosque-university of Al Azhar in Cairo.

When the Protestant missionaries arrived from Europe and America, the number of schools in Egypt greatly increased. Tensions between the Copts and the Protestants also rose. The Western Protestants worked among Muslims too, operating hospitals, schools, and churches; but they felt that the Coptic Christians needed a special evangelistic vigor that they (Protestants) could provide. The Copts, on the other hand, felt that they had done quite well just to survive as Christians over twelve hundred years of conquests. Those Copts who did become Protestants created yet another religious division in Egypt, one which exists to this day.

EGYPTIAN NATIONALISM

Unlike most other minorities in the Middle East, the Copts came to be resented because they had so many important roles in government, and not because they had called for foreign nations to help them. The rise of Egyptian nationalism toward the end of the 1800s created suspicions among the Copts, who feared that Islam was to be the basis of the new movement. Could Copts be loyal Egyptians and support a nationalism that might revive Islam at their expense?

At first the answer was no. Tensions mounted between the small but prestigious Copt minority and their fellow Egyptians. One pasha said openly that Islam in Egypt was in danger because of the increasing number of Copts in government positions.

It is not surprising, then, that many Copts welcomed the British invasion of Egypt in 1882. But Britain's primary concern at the peak of European colonial competition in Asia and Africa was countering the colonial ambitions of France and other European powers. Britain tried to administer Egypt as fairly as possible while furthering her own ambitions. Sensitive to majority opinion in Egypt, Britain reduced the number of Copts employed in government.

If Britain had shown any special favor to the Copts, the history of Egypt and thus the entire Middle East would certainly have been different. British imperialism in Egypt caused the Copts to make a very important decision. In past crises, they had resisted asking for direct intervention on their behalf by outside Christian powers. Now actual British colonial domination over several decades convinced them that long-range security for their faith and their nation depended on active cooperation with their fellow Egyptians.

Until World War I the British occupied Egypt in the face of Ottoman opposition in Istanbul (formerly Constantinople). During the war the Allied advance under General Allenby was through North Africa and Egypt into Palestine. After the war, British control of Egypt was unopposed. Before the Peace Conference convened in Paris, the leading Egyptian nationalists sent their delegation (*Wafd*) to demand immediate independence from Britain, although they wanted to continue a friendly alliance. When this was denied, the *Wafd* became a party, or congress, playing a role similar to that of the Continental Congress during the American Revolution. Its leaders were primarily Muslims and Copts, and its goal was independence: that is, "Egypt for the Egyptians." Never before in Egyptian history had the Crescent and the Cross appeared on the same flag, symbolic of this unique cooperation between Muslims and Christians in building a new nation. Muslim and Coptic leaders paraded arm in arm down the streets of Cairo.

In 1922 the *Wafd* achieved its goal; Britain left Egypt. Two Copts were included in the first Egyptian cabinet. One symbolized the past role of the Coptic minority. He was, as might be expected, Minister of Finance. The other was Foreign Minister, symbolizing a new role that Copts were going to play in twentieth-century Egypt. In the past the Muslims viewed the Copts as interpreters of Western Christian nations to Egyptians. Now Muslims were calling upon their Coptic compatriots to explain Islam and Egypt to the West.

ARAB NATIONALISM

Egyptian nationalism immediately after World War I was not Arab nationalism. Egyptians felt no special ties, other than Islam, with the British-sponsored Hashemites of Trans-Jordan and Iraq nor with Syria and Lebanon. Leaders in Cairo and Alexandria did not look to Damascus or Baghdad for intellectual leadership, but to Paris, London, and Rome.

World War II forced Egypt back into its eternal role as the Western stronghold of the Fertile Crescent. The Americans and English waged a life and death campaign against the Nazi General Rommel (the "Desert Fox"), reminding us that the fate of Europe and the Middle East has always been linked to the great Nile Valley.

Three events after the last World War determined Egypt's return to her role of leadership in the Fertile Crescent. The first was the creation of the League of Arab States in Alexandria (1944); the second was the creation of the state of Israel from parts of Palestine (1948); the third was the nationalization of the Suez Canal by President Gamal Abdel-Nasser in 1955.

The League of Arab States, established under the encouragement of Britain's Prime Minister, Anthony Eden, is a loose association of all Arab states working for greater Arab unity in the midst of traditional disunity. The leadership of this League has always been held by Egypt. In this way Egyptian nationalism became identified with Arab nationalism.

If Egypt ever had second thoughts about her new Arab role, they were destroyed when Israel emerged victorious from the Arab-Israeli war of 1948. Between the two world wars, Egyptians had taken the leadership in verbally protesting Zionist immigration to Palestine.

Now the actual presence of Israel combined with the humiliating defeat of Arab armies created a special bond between Egypt and her neighbors. This bond was cemented by a common Arab feeling that they had been betrayed by the West. The Arab World now looked more than ever to Egypt for leadership against what they called a new kind of Western colonialism.

One of the defeated Egyptian army officers was Major Gamal Abdel-Nasser. In 1952, together with Lt. Colonel Anwar el Sadat, he helped oust King Farouk, the last monarch in a dynasty begun by the illustrious Mohammed Ali. Abdel-Nasser became Prime Minister in 1954 and later President of Egypt. His primary goals were economic development and complete control of Egypt by Egyptians. He did not care whether economic aid came from capitalist or communist countries as long as Egypt's destiny remained in her own hands. The end of the monarchy and the introduction of republican and socialist ideas led to the Government's appropriation of some private lands and wealth which chiefly affected the minority groups.

One of Abdel-Nasser's first acts was to attend the first Afro-Asian conference in Bandung, Indonesia, in April 1955. There he joined other "Third World" leaders in defiance of the idea that weaker nations had to join the capitalist power bloc under American leadership or the Communist bloc under Russia. Egypt saw herself as primarily pro-Egyptian, not pro-capitalist or anti-communist or any other Cold War label. This so-called "Spirit of Bandung" was acclaimed by the Afro-Asian nations at a time when many former European colonies were pushing for independence especially in Indochina and Africa. Abdel-Nasser began putting this spirit to work almost immediately after his return to Cairo.

The late Egyptian President, Gamal Abdel Nasser.

The key to Abdel-Nasser's grand economic design was a new dam on the Nile. He had promised to improve the life of the Egyptian *fellahin* (peasant). America had promised to finance the dam. Five days after the last British soldier left the Suez Canal Zone in June 1955, America, angered over Egyptian overtures to Russia and China (Peking), withdrew this loan to build the dam. Egypt answered by "nationalizing" the Suez Canal, hoping to use its revenues to finance the project. The canal had been founded as an international cooperative a century earlier, but Egypt provided about three-fourths of the canal's expenses. Egypt simply declared the canal Egyptian and continued to operate it as an Egyptian institution.

Egypt's bold action raised her standing tremendously in the eyes of the Third World. On the other hand Britain and France, with strong interests in the Middle East, knew that the nationalization of the canal could mean the crumbling of their power and prestige. France had just been defeated by the Vietnamese but was still fighting the Algerian independence movement. She was very sensitive on this point.

In 1956, Britain, France, and Israel invaded the Suez Canal Zone, taking it by force. At the United Nations, the Soviet Union and the United States in an extraordinary session found themselves agreeing that America's allies were wrong. After Russian threats and American pressures, the three nations withdrew. Gamal Abdel-Nasser emerged as a new hero in the Arab World; indeed he became a symbol of resistance to colonialism for the entire Third World. "Nasserism" came to mean positive neutralism, the refusal to be "pro-West" or "pro-East," and the determination to run one's own country independently. Furthermore, Egypt continued

Wide World Photo

The United Arab Republic with the assistance of the Soviet Union built a high dam at Aswan. This hydropower scheme is among the largest construction projects in Egypt. Shown above is a general view of the Aswan station with waters from the dam rushing through the sluice gates.

to receive assistance from both communist and capitalist countries and has not, as feared, been cut off by the big powers.

EGYPT TODAY

In modern times one does not hear much about the Copts as a separate people because their political destiny has merged with that of other Egyptians. In laying the cornerstone of Cairo's new Coptic Cathedral of St. Mark in 1965, President Abdel-Nasser said, "Islam has recognized Christians as brothers both in the sphere of religion and in the nation."

Soon after 1950, the Coptic Orthodox and Evangelical Churches joined the World Council of Churches. Creative discussions with Islam are also being carried out today in the Arab Republic of Egypt. Many Copts no longer identify with church religion, but remain Copts in their culture and tradition.

To his own people President Gamal Abdel-Nasser was considered the "George Washington" of modern Egypt. He led the struggle against Britain and directed Egypt down her own path. He was the first native-born ruler of Egypt in two thousand years. Many feared that his death in 1970 would cause tremendous change in Egypt and thus in the Middle East. His death was a severe loss to his people but it did not change the basic goals of Egypt now carried out by President Anwar el Sadat. Today the politics and peoples of the Nile Valley remain, as they have for seven thousand years, a dominant force in the life of the Middle East.

QUESTIONS FOR DISCUSSION

1. In what ways are the Copts in Egypt comparable to the American Indians? Why haven't American Indians played the role in America that the Copts have in Egypt?

2. What do you think would have happened if the Copts had sided with the British rather than supporting Egyptian nationalism?

3. In what ways was President Abdel-Nasser the George Washington of modern Egypt? Was he justified in nationalizing the Suez Canal?

4. Can we compare the Jews and Copts as "protected people" under the Moslems to the Amish, Mennonites, and Mormons in America?

III. SHIA ISLAM: AWAITING DIVINE INTERVENTION

And whoso doeth good works, whether male or female, and he or she is a believer, such will enter paradise.

Revealed to the Prophet Mohammed
in The Holy Koran, Chapter IV, v. 124.

ORIGINS

Many men have founded religions; more have fathered nations; the Prophet Mohammed did both within his lifetime. Very soon after his death in 632 A.D., disputes erupted within Islam that created splits lasting until today. The Shia schism was of great importance in the beginnings of Islam. Further divisions created groups like the Assassins, who have become known in the West through popularized literature, and the Baha'is, who emerged from Shia Iran (Persia) in the 1840s. Occasionally, newspapers report that the Aga Khan is visiting his world-wide following of Ismailis, another branch of Shia Islam.

Unlike the Copts, Jews, and Armenians, the Shias are a religious minority who have few ethnic or cultural differences from other Muslims in their own countries.

Today they are the majority only in Iran and Yemen and the largest minority in Iraq. Some live in Syria and Lebanon, while the largest Ismaili communities are in Pakistan.

To understand the Shias we must look at the origins of Islam itself, for the Shias, like most religious minorities, feel themselves to be the true believers carrying on the truth of Islam from its beginnings in the Arabian peninsula.

MOHAMMED AND EARLY ISLAM

Mohammed was born in Mecca around 570 A.D., when this city (in the Arabian peninsula) was a crossroads of highly profitable trade routes used by the Persians, Byzantines, and Abyssinians (Ethiopians). The family or clan, not the individual, was the most important social unit in this Bedouin society. The clan was held together by its need to defend itself and to cooperate in the face of hard desert life. Its head was the appointed sheikh, whose power depended on his people's respect for his age and authority. The word *sheikh* (pronounced "shake") means "old man" in Arabic. A man's total allegiance was to his blood kin. Mohammed was proud to belong to the Hashemite family of the Quarish clan.

Crisscrossing caravans from Egypt, Damascus, and Baghdad had influenced Bedouin tribal religion with smatterings of Jewish and Christian teachings. When Mohammed was about forty, he received an inspiration from the angel Gabriel to speak out about the oneness of God and the wickedness of idolatry. He believed that he was fulfilling or continuing the teachings of Judaism and Christianity. He saw himself as the last in a line of prophets—Abraham, Moses, Jesus—and he probably expected Jews and Christians to rally behind him. Except for one single convert from the Meccan ruling class, Uthman of the Umayya house, his only converts came from the poor. Converts from the poor also included his cousin, Ali. The establishment in Mecca feared perhaps that this new teaching might upset the city's important position in trade. Mohammed's teachings, moreover, incurred the active disapproval of several influential Meccan leaders, and he soon found himself the object of persecution.

Defeated and dejected, Mohammed migrated in 622 A.D., almost 300 miles north to Medina. This move, known as the *Hegira*, marked the birth of a new community, one through which the Middle East became unified. The year 622 marks the beginning of the Islamic calendar because it was the beginning of the Islamic community.

This new religion brought a social revolution. No longer was a person's loyalty to his clan paramount; for a Muslim, family ties were now secondary. This new religion created a community where men of all clans were equal under one God. Blood feuds were suppressed, and a stronger, unified religious community emerged with a higher ethical standard. Mohammed was both the spiritual and political leader. Man could now approach God by "submission." *Islam* is the Arabic word for submission. A person submitted to God by joining the Muslim community as it attempted to realize God's Kingdom on earth. Islam was more than a way to worship; it was a total way of life.

Following a familiar theme, the nomadic desert trader again conquered the sedentary agriculturists and city-dwellers. Only fourteen years after the *Hegira*, Mohammed's followers conquered Damascus (636) and moved eastward to Baghdad and Persia. By 640, Arab armies had conquered Egypt and were slowly moving across North Africa into Spain. However, the successes of Islam suggest other reasons. We know that the rival Persian and Byzantine empires were declining and that the Christian Byzantines so mistreated their minorities that, to the latter, Islam was seen as a welcome liberator. The Arab's tolerance of Christians and Jews made the Arab conquest easier. It seems that the Arabs preferred taxing Christians and Jews to converting them. Indeed, the revenues from these *dhimmi* (protected people) helped finance the growing empire.

But above all, the reason for the Arab victory was the young, simple, and vigorous Islam, united by one faith in one God and by one language—Arabic. Arabic was the language of the Koran, the holy book of Islam, provided by revelations to Mohammed. The importance of this new religion and its ancient language can hardly be exaggerated. Although Arab power was soon supplanted by that of Turks and Persians, Islam and Arabic have remained powerful factors in shaping the Middle East.

THE BEGINNINGS OF SHIISM

Mohammed died only ten years after his *Hegira* to Medina, leaving no sons and no appointed successor. Mohammed's cousin and early supporter, Ali, was also his son-in-law. Because of this close Hashemite family tie, some suggested that Ali was the rightful *Caliph* (Arabic for "successor"). This group was called Ali's "Party" (*Shia* in Arabic). But others felt that the aging Abu-Bakr was more devoted to Islam and insisted that faith was more important than family ties. Ali lost to Abu-Bakr who became the First Caliph (See pp. 64, 65) but he died within a year. The more vigorous Omar succeeded him and within eleven years conquered Syria, Egypt, Iraq, and Persia in the name of Islam. Omar's death renewed an old feud between the Hashemite and the Umayyid families. Again Ali lost, but in the year, 656, when the victorious Uthman was murdered, Ali became Caliph for the last five years of his life.

The question of succession continued, as Ali's followers, the Shias, insisted that the next Caliph had to be related to Mohammed through Ali. When the Caliphate once more went to the Umayyid family, the Shias might have disappeared altogether had Ali's son not been massacred with his followers at Karbala. The blood of these martyrs became the seed of a new Shia determination to rally behind Ali's family as the legitimate heirs of the Caliphate. Thus a split developed, and the Shias grew apart from the main Islamic stream, the Sunni tradition.

It may appear that Shiism arose more from family feud and political controversy than from disagreement over religious doctrine, but we must recall that in Islam religion and politics are indivisible. In the beginning there was little difference between Sunni and Shia theology. Both groups should pray five times daily, observe the month of fasting, give alms to the poor, and make pilgrimages to Mecca or other holy cities. These four pillars of Islam are essentially the same in Sunni and Shia Islam. But in the first pillar, or duty, the Shia Muslims differed from the Sunnis. Reciting the "Word of Witness," the Sunnis declare, "There is no God but God and Mohammed is his Prophet." The Shias add, ". . . . and Ali is the vice-regent of God."

The Caliph, or *Imam*, as the Shias called him, soon became more important than the Koran itself. The Imam was regarded as infallible, a superhuman power

THE FIRST CALIPHS OF ISLAM AND THE SUNNI-SHIA SPLIT

Roman numerals number Mohammed's successors (Caliphs).
Single line indicates kinship ties; double line signifies
spiritual succession of caliphate.

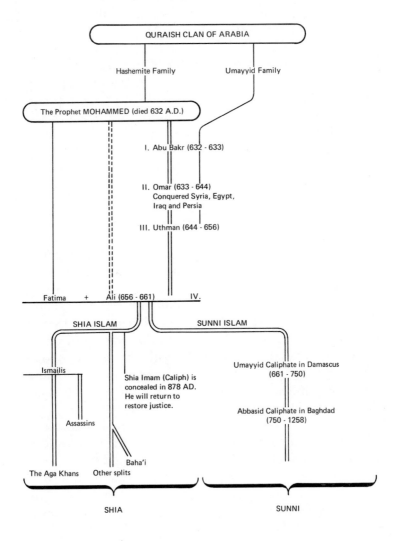

MUSLIM BELIEFS

The five duties of a Muslim:		
	1 Recitation of the Word of Witness	"THERE IS ONLY ONE GOD AND MOHAMMED IS HIS PROPHET" (Shias add, "And Ali is the vice-regent of God") A person becomes a Muslim by reciting and believing this most powerful sentence in Islam. The unity of God: Creator of all King of the Day of Judgement. All things are by His decree Transcendent and sovereign. Has ninety-nine attributes or names—Beneficent, Merciful. . . . Mohammed, The greatest of the prophets: Other prophets are also important—Abraham, Moses, Jesus. . . The Holy Koran revealed to him, the final scripture Ethics founded on his deeds
	2 Saying the stated prayers daily	Five periods daily. Always includes the first chapter of the Koran. Worshipper must wash face, hands, and feet before praying. Muslims used to face Jerusalem while praying but now face Mecca. Most important on Fridays and best done in a mosque.
	3 Fasting: especially the month Ramadan	No liquids (including water) and no eating or smoking from sunrise to sunset. Illness exempts the faithful. Ramadan follows lunar year.
	4 Giving the legal alms	Giving alms to the poor was instituted and encouraged by the Prophet Mohammed, especially at times of good fortune, births, weddings, holidays. Alms used to be collected like taxes but is now purely voluntary.
	5 Pilgrimage to Mecca or Karbala	For most Muslims (Sunni) a pilgrimmage should be made to Mecca before death. Shias often go to Karbala in Iraq where Ali's son and his followers were massacred.

having fallen on his shoulders from God through Mohammed. Any day God might speak to his community or reveal himself in some other way. In the fullness of time the righteous but defeated people of Ali, the Shias, would return to power and establish justice. The Shias looked to divine intervention to solve oppression and injustice.

THE GOLDEN AGE OF ISLAM

The Umayyad Caliphate in Damascus (Syria) was destroyed in 750, not by Shia power but by internal revolts by mostly non-Arab Moslems, who resented the Caliphate's favor of Arabs over others within Islam. This was contrary to the Koran's teaching. The Shias encouraged these dissidents to overthrow their oppressive rulers. Indeed there was an immediacy about Shiism that attracted the underdogs—a hope that sustained the oppressed. The overthrow of the Umayyids in Damascus, though not a direct victory for the Shias, helped spread Shia ideas. A new Caliphate moved to Baghdad under the Abbasid family. Although the Abbasids were also Sunni, Islam was no longer controlled by Arabs alone. Non-Arab Muslims with Shia ideas, and Persian concepts about the divine nature of rulers, injected new strength and mysticism into the Shia cause.

The Abbasids in Baghdad focused on internal development rather than expansion, and they brought Islamic civilization to its peak. The period from 900-1200 A.D., was Islam's Golden Age, with Baghdad its cultural center. The mixture of Arabs, Persians, and Turks and the contributions of Sunni and Shia Muslims, Jews, Christians, and Zoroastrians encouraged the flourishing of art, philosophy, mathematics, trade, and religion. The city of Mosul (ancient Nineveh) was another great center along the Tigris on the trade route to Aleppo in Syria. The word *muslin*, designating the finest cottons, comes from Mosul, today one of Iraq's largest cities.

But success brought the luxury of internal dissent, and the same diversity that had helped make Baghdad the cultural center of Europe, Africa, and the Middle East became responsible for its decline at about the time that the first Norsemen set foot on North American soil.

SHIISM IN EGYPT AND MESOPOTAMIA

About the year 990, one claimant to the Shia Imamate living in Syria gathered enough forces to take North Africa from the Abbasids who had ruled for 150 years. Claiming to have re-established the house of Ali, he began a new rival dynasty, naming it "Fatimid" after Mohammed's daughter, the wife of Ali. The Fatimids ruled Egypt and later Syria. The wealth, splendor, and intellectual vigor of Egypt under Shia rule have become legendary. The Mosque-University of Al Ahzar was founded in Cairo at that time. And it was then that Shia converts formed new sects like the Druzes (who later moved to Lebanon).

The Shias under Fatimid power competed with Abbasid Baghdad rather than uniting Islam against her external enemies. In fact, the Shias of Egypt belonged to a more radical branch of Shiism called "Ismailiism." Ismaili missionaries went from Egypt to Iraq and Persia winning many converts among the masses who were more than ready to be convinced that the Sunni leadership in Baghdad was corrupt.

Indeed, by about 950, a Persian family with Shia sympathies held the real power in Baghdad but allowed the Sunni Abbasids to maintain their Caliph. By the end of the tenth century, then, it looked as if the Shias might dominate the Islamic world, but the Seljuk Turks from the Northeast and the Crusaders from the West threatened the collapse of Islam itself. The Seljuks, however, became Sunni Muslims themselves and spread the faith with their new conquests. The Shias, in the face of the Crusaders and Seljuks, continued to struggle in the name of Islam as they interpreted it.

THE ASSASSIN FEDAYEEN

At this time (1100) a zealous Ismaili sect seized fortresses in Persia and Syria, in a man-to-man guerrilla-like struggle that frightened Sunni leaders and terrified the Crusaders. This sect had a "Robin Hood" image for the masses of poor who looked on with awe as it publicly murdered nobles and government officials in the name of religious devotion.

Crusader accounts have led us to believe that members of this sect took hashish (*cannabis indica*) to prepare themselves for their deadly deeds. In fact, this was the origin of the English word "assassin." But it is more likely that the hashish was used as part of young men's initiations into the sect. On a drug-induced high, the men were said to be taken into a beautiful garden and to be surrounded by beautiful young women. When they came to themselves, their leader promised the young men that such a paradise could be theirs forever if they became his devoted *fedayeen*. This word in Arabic means "those who give their lives," and the fedayeen did just that. Sent on a mission to assassinate an enemy, they never thought of returning alive. Giving their own lives was part of this sacrificial act in the name of their faith. The Assassins were feared and revered during the time of the Crusades by Crusader and Sunni Moslem alike. It is no coincidence that the term fedayeen has since been used to refer to Armenian freedom fighters, Palestinian commandos, or in fact any person ready to sacrifice his life for his cause.

SALADIN, THE MONGOLS, AND THE OTTOMANS

But it was not in the fate of the Shias to oust the Sunnis. Saladin, a Kurd by origin, marched into Egypt after defeating the Crusaders in Palestine and restored Fatimid Egypt to the Sunni fold in 1171.

Then in 1258, the grandson of Ghengis Khan sacked Baghdad, dramatically ending the Abbasid Caliphate. The Mongols looted Baghdad's riches, slew or scattered its sages, traders, and poets, and reduced it in a day of terror from the center of Islam to a minor outpost of the illustrious Mongol Empire. The most disastrous act by the Mongols was the destruction of the delicate Tigris-Euphrates irrigation system dating to Babylonian times. Not even today, with the help of modern technology, has this system been fully restored.

Islamic armies stopped the Mongol advance at Goliath Springs in 1260 (see Chap. I, p. 23). Unfortunately the Mongols are remembered for their acts of destruction rather than for their own cultural and artistic contributions to world civilization.

The Ottoman Empire became the champion of Sunni Islam by the fourteenth century. It is not surprising that some discontented minorities soon challenged the Ottomans by rallying under the banner of the Shia faith. By uniting with the Shia Safavid family in Persia, they were able to challenge seriously the Sunni Ottomans. For three hundred years the Shias in the area we today call Iraq were a "Third World" caught between Persian and Ottoman ambitions. Every Ottoman invasion brought persecution; every Persian counter-invasion restored their hope. By the sixteenth century one-third of the eastern end of the Fertile Crescent and most of Persia was Shia, as it is today. Nevertheless, the Ottomans gained final military control from Persia of the area known today as Iraq.

The Shias remained a minority in Syria and other parts of the Ottoman domains. It is ironical that Sunni Islam protected Christians and Jews as the Koran demanded, while Shias, "heretics" within the Moslem faith, were persecuted. In order to protect themselves from the Sunni authorities, most Shias in Syria and Lebanon settled in mountains and valleys where they could effectively defend themselves.

SHIISM TODAY

In Iraq, Shia Islam had attracted the poorer peasants in the south. By the twentieth century it was Iraq's largest minority because the Sunni Moslems were divided into Arabs and Kurds. The Kurds were neither Arab nor Turk, and wanted their own state. At the close of World War I, Shias were among the nationalist leaders demanding an independent Iraqi state.

Between the wars Arab nationalism was on the rise in Iraq as well as in the rest of the Middle East. The Sunnis wanted Iraq to be part of a larger Pan-Arab state with emphasis on "Arabness" rather than on religion; but this left out the non-Arab Sunni Kurds. The Shias were afraid that pan-Arabism would really mean Pan-Islamism, leaving them a smaller minority sect in a Sunni federation of all Arab states. The Shias wanted Iraq to be an independent state in which all Iraqis would be equal under the law.

Iraq became a constitutional monarchy in 1924 under King Feisal I. The monarchies of Iraq and Jordan remained closely linked through Hashemite family ties. General Abdul Karim Kassem, who led the revolt in 1958 in which Feisal II was killed, declared Iraq part of "the Arab nation." He became premier of a new republic, turned away from commitments which had been made to America and looked instead toward the Soviet Union. On the day after his revolution, American marines landed in Lebanon and British troops in Jordan, both at the request of the pro-Western governments of those two countries which feared similar revolts. Some American leaders looked upon the already formed United Arab Republic (a union of Syria and Egypt) as too friendly to the Soviet Union and feared that Iraq's move in the same direction might result in a unification of these three influential Arab states. Thus under the "Eisenhower Doctrine" of the mid-1950s, the United States had pledged support to defend friendly Middle Eastern states from direct or indirect communist aggression.

American policy has not been based on a uniform or comprehensive understanding of the Middle East. It has often been more concerned with keeping communism out of the Middle East rather than with a positive commitment to the area. It has had an anti-communist focus rather than a specific positive commitment. Since no Arab countries have experienced Chinese or Russian domination but all of them have had a history of European rule, it is not surprising that Arab nationalists tend to express anti-Western feelings by experimenting with socialist ideas.

Today the most active minority group in Iraq is the

Kurds, but the Shias remain the largest single minority. Their faith unites them with Iran to the East where Shia Islam is not only the dominant faith, but also the most unifying factor in a nation with people of Turkish, Arab, Parsi, Afghan, and other origins.

Lebanon today is almost equally divided between Christians and Muslims. The Shia Muslims are recognized and incorporated into Lebanon's unique inclusion by law of minorities into government. Lebanon's President is traditionally a Maronite Christian, her Premier a Sunni Muslim, and the Speaker of the Chamber of Deputies a Shia.

The world leader of the Ismaili sect, His Highness Aga Khan I, was born in Iran in 1800 but was exiled to India in 1840 where he sought British protection for all Ismailis. His grandson, Aga Khan III, was educated in Iran and Europe but maintained his Indian citizenship. During World War I he called upon his subjects to support Britain unreservedly. After the war he represented India at the League of Nations, becoming its president in 1937. His grandson, Aga Khan IV, is the spiritual head of all Ismailis today—their closest living link to the Prophet Mohammed through Ali. Aga Khan IV was born in Geneva in 1936 and completed his studies at Harvard in 1959. He makes frequent trips to Ismaili communities in Malaya, Burma, India, Afghanistan, Iran, Syria, Yemen, Morocco, and East Africa.

But the majority of Shias believe that the last Imam concealed himself in 878 A.D., and will return in the fullness of time. Many pretenders have appeared from time to time, proclaiming themselves as the long-awaited Imam or one of his prophets. The most illustrious case in recent years was the claim of a young Persian, Mirza Ali Muhammad, to be the promised Imam of the Shias. Most

Shias rejected him because he could not show the supernatural signs associated with the Imam. After his martyrdom in Tabriz in 1850, his following increased, and his beliefs became the foundation of the Baha'i faith which has spread rapidly in the twentieth century. The three principal Baha'i temples are in Wilmette, Illinois, Turkestan, Russia, and Haifa, Israel.

We have seen that the whole history of Islam has been deeply influenced by thirteen centuries of rivalry between the Sunni and Shia parties stemming from a split in Islam after the death of Mohammed. With its many branches developed over the years, Shiism remains an important aspect of the religion and politics of the Muslim world today.

QUESTIONS FOR DISCUSSION

1. What beliefs do Islam, Judaism, and Christianity hold in common?

2. Why were the Shias not tolerated by the Sunnis, while Jews and Christians were?

3. Do you know of any modern parallels to the Assassins' religious use of drugs? What about their religious sanction for murder?

4. Do some research on the Black Muslims in the United States. How are they similar to Shia and Sunni Muslims? How do they differ?

IV. THE JEWS: PEOPLE OF THE BOOK

What does the Lord require of you but to do justice and to love kindness, and to walk humbly with your God.

The Prophet Micah (VI:8)

PATRIARCHAL PERIOD

About 1900 B.C., Abraham and his family migrated westward from the Sumerian city of Ur, following the fertile areas at least as far as Syria-Palestine, where he became the father of many nations. Genesis records his encounter with the King of Salem (probably Jerusalem) and the accounts of Abraham's sons, Ishmael and Isaac, and their families. Ravaged by famine and the rivalry between the Hittites and Egyptians, Isaac's descendents emigrated to the more fertile Nile Valley sometimes between 1700 and 1300 B.C. Though they lived in peace under the dynasty of Hiksos, under the later Pharaohs of Thebes the Hebrews found themselves enslaved and persecuted beyond endurance.

After breaking out of this captivity into the Sinai Desert, the Hebrews led by the young Moses made a covenant or agreement with their God. In return for obedience to the Ten Commandments, God promised them land and prosperity.

FIRST HEBREW COMMONWEALTH

Under the leadership of Joshua, the Hebrews conquered parts of Canaan around 1200 B.C. Settling down comfortably in this fertile land which they believed was promised to them by God, many began to worship the agricultural and fertility gods of the locality. Threats from the Philistines united them with new vigor under King Saul, who in the name of their God, established the Kingdom of Israel around 100 B.C. His successor, David, expanded the kingdom, conquering Jerusalem and moving the capital there from Shiloh. The importance of Jerusalem to the Jews dates from this time. Disputes after the death of David's son Solomon (930 B.C.) divided the kingdom into Israel in the north, with its capital in Samaria, and Judah in the south, with its capital in Jerusalem.

This split weakened the Hebrew nation at a time when Assyrian, Babylonian, and Egyptian powers surrounded them. In 721 B.C., Samaria fell to the Assyrians and northern Israel was largely absorbed into the peoples of the Middle East, becoming the so-called "Lost Tribes of Israel." A small group of Samaritans exists today in Israel.

Judah, however, became a typical "Third World" power. The people of Judah did not want to join either Egypt or Babylonia, but they knew from experience that they had better side with the stronger if they were to survive. Though the prophet Jeremiah urged siding with Babylonia, majority opinion favored Egypt. But when, in 586 B.C., the Babylonians under Nebuchadnezzar beseiged Jerusalem, the hoped-for Egyptian help never came. Judah fell, and some of its people (Jews, as they were thereafter called) found refuge in Egypt. A few stayed in Judah under Babylonian rule, but most went to Babylon, taking their sacred books that contained their law and the foundations of their faith.

One of the most important contributions of the ancient Middle East to the world was monotheism—an enduring contribution by the Hebrew people and indeed the cornerstone of Christianity and Islam. Even though the Hebrew prophets were despised in their own lifetime, they transformed tribal ritualism into ethical concepts which have influenced every kind of human relationship in the Middle East and in the West. God's basic demand as they interpreted it was not to fulfill formal ritual or engage in pretentious sacrifice but to do justice, love mercy, and walk humbly with God.

While the origin of the Hebrews, the Arabs, and others is traced to Abraham, and the beginning of their monotheistic faith to Moses, the origins of the Jewish people date from the destruction of Judah in 586. For centuries after this, Jews saw themselves as a people of God rather than a geographically defined nation. They followed Jeremiah's advice to contribute to the building of whatever city they inhabited. Wherever they were, Jews refashioned their institutions, reinterpreted their ancient literature, and lived by their law (Torah). Many hoped to return to the land of their forefathers. It was at this time that the concept of a messiah entered Jewish belief in any significant way. He was to be a deliverer from suffering and a restorer of the greatness of Israel. Many practiced their faith with the expectation that the messiah might come at any time.

THE SECOND COMMONWEALTH

The hope of return was fulfilled in the lifetime of some exiled Jews. The Persian conquest of Babylon in 539 B.C. freed the Jews to return to Jerusalem. Within twenty-three years the Jews had rebuilt their Temple, but along with other minorities in Syria-Palestine they continued to be a "Third World" people caught between competing empires. As we noted in the first chapters, Alexander the Great in the name of Greece took these lands from Persia in about 330 B.C. After his death, the Ptolemies of Egypt and the Seleucids of Syria-Palestine struggled for the inheritance of Alexander's domains. Some Jews again favored siding with Egypt; others preferred the Seleucids. A successful revolt against all forms of Greek domination was led by a group of Jews called the Maccabees. For almost a century the Jews ruled themselves in Palestine.

But fratricidal wars once more gave way to a new foreign invasion when the great Roman Empire invaded the area in 63 B.C., making Judah the Roman province of Judea. The birth of Christianity was of little consequence to the Romans and Jews who were busy struggling against each other. Two Jewish parties emerged with different opinions about how to adjust to their latest conquerors. The Saducees were the aristocrats, the high officials who were less interested in resisting Rome as long as the Temple remained intact. The Pharisees were stricter religiously and were openly opposed to Roman rule. They put more emphasis on written laws and oral traditions. One wing of the Pharisees, the Zealots, took up arms against Rome. When Rome besieged Jerusalem in 70 A.D., many Jews wanted to surrender, but the Zealots fought to the end and Jerusalem was destroyed. A small fort at nearby Masada held out a few more days until the last man was killed. Masada has become famous among Jews as a symbol of resistance—a "Jewish Alamo."

JEWS IN THE MIDDLE EAST

The Romans exiled the Jews from Palestine and destroyed their Second Temple. Parts of it are preserved as the "Wailing Wall" in Jerusalem today. With the Temple gone, traditional sacrifice and the priesthood also died; but rabbis (teachers) preserved the law, and synagogues sprang up wherever Jews were, once more preserving the spirit of Judaism in other lands.

Many Jews chose their former Babylonian "prison" as a refuge in exile. Others joined the Jewish community in Egypt or stayed in the Syria-Palestine area. As Christianity grew in the Eastern Roman (Byzantine) Empire, Judaism had to struggle to survive. Laws limited Jewish participation in the civil, political, and cultural life of the Christian Byzantine world. Jews were forbidden to build new synagogues or repair old ones. In 629, the Christian Emperor Heraclius massacred many of the Jewish residents of Jerusalem. It is not surprising that Jewish emigration to the Tigris-Euphrates river valley increased, making Baghdad the world center of Judaism for the next five hundred years. There the Babylonian Talmud ("Teachings") was compiled, bringing together all of Hebrew wisdom from the Hebrew Bible until 500 A.D. The spread of this Talmud to other Jewish centers throughout the world shaped the modern soul of Judaism and was a very important factor in Jewish survival. The Jews became known as the "People of the Book" because of the importance of the Hebrew Bible and the Talmud.

The Arab conquest of the seventh century helped spread the Talmud to other Jewish communities in the Middle East and Europe. That the Arabs were able to conquer such a large part of the world in only forty years was due in part to the discontent of all the minorities under Byzantine rule. One Jewish document calls Mohammed's new religion an act of God's mercy. It is true that Muslim armies were fighting a holy war (*jihad*) for Islam, but the image of conversions forced by the sword are incorrect, especially with regard to the Jews and Christians. These two minorities were regarded by Muslim law as *dhimmi* ("protected people"), and pagans were encouraged to become Jews or Christians if they refused to become Muslims. Jewish and Christian minorities had much to gain from the Arab conquests. The Zoroastrians of Persia were sometimes treated as protected people also. As in all previous conquests, the minorities were heavily taxed, but now Jews could live anywhere and could open schools. Jews could pray in their synagogues without fear. Slowly Jewish learning revived even in Syria-Palestine, where persecution by Christians had been heaviest.

The two most important centers for Jews remained Baghdad and Egypt. No other part of the Middle East could compete with Baghdad after the rise of the Abbasid Caliphate (see Chapter III) and the Islamic Renaissance which centered there.

Some Islamic scholars considered it providential that the Islamic Renaissance blossomed in the very capitals where there were large Jewish communities. In fact, by 1000 A.D., Jews spoke Arabic and practiced their religion within the Arabic culture of the time. Many

Jewish and Christian scientists, mathematicians, artists, and philosophers contributed to what is called the Golden Age of Islam. Furthermore, Plato, Aristotle, and Euclid were read in Arabic by Jewish scholars for the first time. Jews and other minorities taught their children their own tongues, especially for religious purposes, but they used grammars written in Arabic. In Baghdad the chief rabbi of the Jewish community was a favored member of the court of the Caliph. Thus Islam contributed greatly to the development of Jewish literature, language, and philosophy, while Jews contributed equally to the Golden Age of Islam.

JEWS IN THE WEST

When the Mongols and Turks challenged Arab supremacy in the thirteenth century, the Jewish center of learning shifted from Baghdad to Muslim Spain. The most famous Talmudic scholar of the Islamic period was Maimonides (1135-1204). This Spanish-born Jew was recognized after his death in Egypt as one of the greatest scholars of the Middle Ages.

Other Jews were also making many contributions to European culture during the Middle Ages. However, their marginal life in Europe presented a striking contrast to their full involvement in life under Islam.

Between the thirteenth and eighteenth centuries in Europe, the Talmud was often condemned and burned in public places. Partly because Jews were held responsible by some Christians for the death of Christ, their European history was punctuated by a series of expulsions, plunders, and massacres. Nothing illustrates better the plight of Jews in both Europe and the Middle East than the European Crusades, beginning in the twelfth

Wide World Photo

Crowds fill the plaza beside the Wailing Wall in Jerusalem to celebrate the Harvest Festival.

century, into the heart of the Mediterranean world. Although the holy places had been accessible to pilgrims of all faiths under Arab Muslim domination, the newer converts to Islam, the Turks, began to limit European passage into Syria-Palestine. Christian Europe mounted the Crusades for many reasons—to retaliate against the Turks, to contain Islam, to gain spiritual merits for Christians, to search for economic markets, and even to be a military arm of Papal foreign policy. Whatever the Crusades were to Europeans, they were a disaster to the non-Christian communities of the Middle East and even to some Christian communities like the Copts (See Chapter II).

No one group suffered more than the Jews, who were targets of the crusading spirit both in Europe and the Middle East. Undisciplined mobs massacred Jews in cities along the Rhine as part of the first Crusade (1096), while later massacres took place in England during the third Crusade of Richard the Lion-Hearted (1157-99).

In their zeal to conquer the lands of the Bible, the Crusaders slaughtered many peoples of the Middle East, especially Jews and Muslims. After the initial conquests, small Crusader states set up in the Middle East became little trading post empires.

Many Jews in Europe had been forced by discriminatory laws into becoming merchants and traders. The trade monopoly they held with the Mediterranean world was broken by the Crusades, as a new class of merchant-traders emerged among Christians. These new merchants, particularly those in Venice and Genoa, profited enormously from trade with Christian Crusader states along the coast of Syria-Palestine.

Even the defeat of the Crusaders by Saladin and

their expulsion by the Mamluks of Egypt had dire consequences for the Jews. In retaking the coastal area, the Muslims killed thousands of Christians and Jews. The experience of the Jews in this clash between Islam and Christianity is typical of the perennial problem for minorities—survival depends on cooperating with those in power, but that cooperation itself endangers survival when power changes hands. Thus the Jews were killed by Crusaders who considered them pro-Muslim and then were slaughtered by Muslims for being supposedly pro-Crusader.

When Christian Europe completed its conquest of Spain from Islam in 1492, all Jews were expelled along with Muslims (Moors) as infidels. The first Jews to come to America may have sailed that same year with Columbus, but most went to the leading cities of Europe and the Middle East. By the early 1500s, they were relegated by law to inferior sections of European cities. It is no coincidence that the word *ghetto* itself is of European origin, first applied to Jewish quarters in Italy. The French Revolution (1789) brought the first real hope to European Jews; but even in the nineteenth and twentieth centuries, Jews in the West have never known what to expect. As a general pattern, the Jews were welcomed at first by Western nations eager to build their strength in an era of nationalism and overseas expansion. During times of prosperity, welcome turned to moderate toleration. In periods of crisis, toleration often suddenly shifted to persecution. But in the midst of all this, Jewish thinkers contributed spectacularly to the Western technological revolution. And they created a revolution within Judaism itself which continuously adapted the ancient faith to the modern world.

JEWS UNDER THE OTTOMAN EMPIRE

While Europe was busy colonizing the New World, the Ottoman Turks gained control of the Middle East and Southeastern Europe. The Arabs, now divided into locally powerful family dynasties, were under Ottoman rule from Istanbul. Arab political power was gone, but Islam had become more powerful than ever under a new Ottoman imperial system (Chapters I and III). The Jews lived in their own *millets* as did other cultural-religious minorities, with their own local autonomy and representatives in Istanbul who spoke on their behalf. A Portuguese Jew named Nasi, for example, was a close advisor to Sultan Sulaiman the Magnificent in the fifteenth century. There were small communities of Jews throughout the Ottoman lands, but the largest and most influential were in the largest cities—Cairo, Damascus, Aleppo, Mosul, Baghdad—the great provincial capitals and commercial centers of the Ottoman world.

In Iraq, for example, Jews were in parliament and government service as well as in the army and private business. Their success in business, however, created a kind of envy and mistrust which became translated into religious animosity. Christian and other minorities which were economically successful under the Ottoman system were equally mistrusted (See Chapters II and V), especially in the nineteenth century when they were suspected of collaborating with European colonial interests.

Indeed, it was the rise of European colonialism that altered the economic and political face of the four-hundred-year-old Ottoman Empire and forced the Middle East to join a Western-dominated world. Since 1850, it has been impossible to talk about changes in the Middle

East, particularly with reference to the Jews, without talking about events in Europe.

ANTI-JUDAISM AND ZIONISM

Around 1890, the world Jewish population was estimated to be nine million, seven and a half million of whom were in Europe. About 150 thousand lived in the Turkish and Arab provinces of the Ottoman Empire under Sultan Abdul Hamid II.

Jews, Arabs, and Ethiopians who speak Amharic are called Semites because their original language was Semitic. Since Jews had been the only Semites in Europe for centuries, prejudice against Jews was called anti-Semitism. Organized massacres of Jews which were called "pogroms" occurred periodically in Europe. Since most of the European Jews lived in Russia, the word pogrom originated there; yet anti-Semitism was equally present in Western Europe. In the name of Pan-Slavism, Russia also carried out pogroms against other non-Slavic peoples in her empire.

The rise of Jewish nationalism was sparked by a combination of many factors. First there were Jews who for centuries had dreamed and written about returning to their "Promised Land" in Palestine. Then there were Russian Jews who fled the pogroms of the late nineteenth century. Many came to America, but some decided to set up Jewish colonies in Palestine organized on socialist principles. By 1882, Sultan Abdul Hamid outlawed this type of colonizing experiment.

Third, the Zionist movement united the ancient Jewish dream of returning to Zion with actual Jewish immigration to Palestine. In 1896, Theodor Herzl, a brilliant Austrian journalist, became the father of modern political Zionism by writing his famous book *The Jewish State* as a response to the anti-Semitism he had witnessed in Western Europe. In this book he hypothesized that Jews and non-Jews could never really live together in peace and concluded that a Jewish State should be created. Others equally passionate joined him and began the struggle for the creation of a Jewish state in Palestine if possible, or elsewhere if necessary. Herzl was unable to obtain Sultan Abdul Hamid's consent for this project, but his vision was taken over by the World Zionist Organization which pursued the idea of Palestine as the natural site for a Jewish homeland.

The rise of modern political Zionism coincided with the rise of European colonialism. Zionist leaders went to European capitals seeking support for Zionist goals in Palestine. The German Kaiser was unreceptive, but Britain proposed that a section of her own East African empire would be considered for the Jewish homeland. Finally in 1917 as part of British strategy in World War I, Lord Balfour declared British support for the idea (See Chapter I, pp. 39, 41, and 42).

While Palestine remained under British mandate between the world wars, Zionists were led to believe that Britain was serious about increasing Jewish settlement there. Palestinian Arabs reminded Britain, on the other hand, that the Balfour Declaration offered support for a Jewish home in Palestine only if the rights of non-Jews were guaranteed. As World War II approached, refugees from Nazi Germany exerted extreme pressure for more Jewish settlement. The British, caught between increasing pressure from both Zionists and Palestinians, were paying the price for making conflicting promises to both parties. Each of the three groups saw the other two as conspiring against its own aims.

The refusal of Britain to open wide the doors of Palestine at this critical moment led to an all-out revolt by the Zionists in mandated Palestine. To become commandos in an underground war against the British was a very difficult decision inasmuch as Britain was fighting against Hitler's Nazi Germany. Paradoxically, Jewish guerrillas fought the British in Palestine while the Zionist movement supported Britain's war against Germany.

Thus, modern Zionism rode into the Middle East on the shoulders of nineteenth-century colonialism. Within a generation, however, it had scrambled down, taken up the rifle, and become one of the first post-World War II movements of liberation against a European colonial power. The struggle against Britain, however, was short-lived compared to the prolonged war Israel has been waging ever since with her Arab neighbors.

After the close of World War II, Britain announced her proposed withdrawal from Palestine (set for May 1948) and turned over the whole question to the United Nations. Already England, America, and other Western nations had sent numerous study commissions to Palestine, but the years immediately after the war were to see many more. Refugees, as might be suspected, were more interested in survival than in commission reports. Jews poured into Palestine from war-ravaged Europe. Accounts of millions of Jews massacred by Germans and thousands of destitute survivors moved many statesmen and organizations to untiring action on their behalf. By 1946, there were six hundred thousand Jews in Palestine, three-fifths of whom had come from Europe. After the implementation of the Zionist program, many would

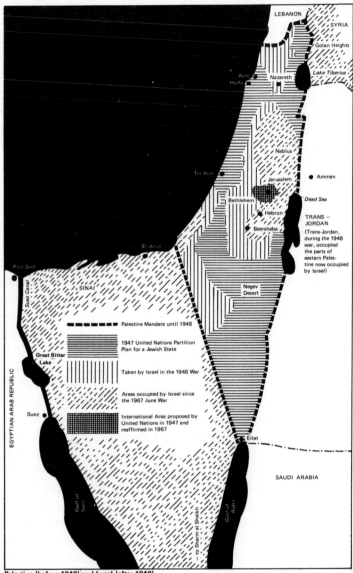

LEBANON

SYRIA

Golan Heights

Acre
Haifa   Nazareth   *Lake Tiberius*

Nablus

Tel Aviv •

Jerusalem   • Amman

Bethlehem   *Dead Sea*

Hebron

Beersheba

TRANS –
JORDAN
(Trans-Jordan,
during the 1948
war, occupied
the parts of
eastern Pales-
tine now occupied
by Israel)

El Arish

Port Said

SINAI

Negev
Desert

**Great Bitter
Lake**

—————— Palestine Mandate until 1948

1947 United Nations Partition
Plan for a Jewish State

Taken by Israel in the 1948 War

Areas occupied by Israel since
the 1967 June War

International Area proposed by
United Nations in 1947 and
reaffirmed in 1967

Suez •

• Eilat

SAUDI ARABIA

*Gulf of
Suez*

*Gulf of
Aqaba*

— to Sharm al Sheikh

EGYPTIAN ARAB REPUBLIC

Palestine (before 1948) and Israel (after 1948)

come from Middle Eastern countries, especially Iraq.

After Britain announced that all responsibility for Palestine would be given to the United Nations, the General Assembly proposed a solution on November 29, 1947, by voting to divide the mandate into Jewish and Arab states. Jerusalem was to continue the special status it had under the Ottomans but would be under international supervision. The Palestine Arabs reacted as predicted (see Chapter VI). Riots led to more violence and by spring of 1948, war had broken out between the Zionists and the Arab armies of Egypt and Jordan. Although greatly outnumbered, the Jewish forces pushed back the Arabs and occupied parts of the mandate intended for the Palestinian state by the United Nations partition plan. Zionist forces held one-half of Jerusalem, the other half (the Old City) being occupied by the army of Trans-Jordan, which also held what remained of the former Palestine.

CREATION OF ISRAEL

Although the United Nations partition plan was a failure, Israel was proclaimed an independent nation on May 14, 1948, by her first Premier, David Ben-Gurion. President Truman recognized the new state immediately. Young and full of enthusiasm and optimism, Israel developed rapidly with generous support from her friends. In her politics, government, and economy, she is very much like Western nations. Her adanced technology and her agricultural triumph over the parched desert areas (Negev) have served as models for other developing countries.

Although religious differences in Israel create problems, Jewishness interpreted non-religiously remains

the unifying cement of Zionism throughout the world.
Today, Zionists consider the following to be their goals:
the unity of the Jewish people with Israel as their center;
the ingathering of the "exiles" (as they call Jews outside
Israel) from all countries of the world; the strengthening
of Israel; the preservation of the identity of the people
through fostering of Jewish and Hebrew education and
spiritual and cultural values; and the protection of
Jewish rights everywhere. In short, Zionism looks upon
Israel as the spiritual home and modern frontier for Jews
everywhere in the world.

That Israel has internal problems is understandable
in light of her large Arab minorities and the great influx
of Jews from almost every nation in the world. Sixty
percent of Israel's 2.5 million Jews are of Middle Eastern
origin—mostly from Iraq, Yemen, and North Africa.
Nevertheless the power of the establishment in Israel is
concentrated in the hands of Jews from the West
(Europe, America, and South Africa).

But Israel also has a major external problem. Since
1948, she has been at war with her Arab neighbors. Will
she be able to come to peace terms with them? Four
problems stand in the way. The most crucial is the question of the thousands of Palestinian refugees who have
lost their homes since 1947 (See Chapter VI). Second,
there is the question of the surrounding Arab nations.
Third, there has never been agreement among those
Jews in Israel (over two million) and those Jews living in
Russia, America, Europe, and the rest of the world
(about twelve million) on the Zionist program. Some
American Jews, for instance, do not accept Israel's claiming to speak for them. And finally, Israel is torn by
internal disagreement over the approach to the first two
questions. Some Israelis who are not Zionists feel that

Palestinians should return to Israel and become part of a secular state which will cooperate with the Arab states. Others want Israel to remain a predominantly Jewish state, with its minorities represented as they now are in the Knesset, or Parliament. There are many more viewpoints in Israel's debate over the best path to permanent peace, but they all relate in one way or another to the problems raised by displaced Palestinians and the hostility of surrounding Arab nations.

Whatever the intellectual arguments within Israel, and between Israel and Jews in other countries, events in the Middle East between 1948 and the present have often depended on decisions that Israel has felt obliged to make at moments when she has felt her very existence threatened. Non-Jews must understand this in order to understand Israeli psychology.

In both 1956 and 1967, Israel felt threatened enough to mobilize her armed forces. It is hard for non-Israelis to visualize this, for every able-bodied male and female in Israel, every truck, indeed every part of the society is involved in defense. What happens once Israel is mobilized for war? She must either sit around waiting for the Arab regular armies to move, or she must attack swiftly. To wait is to lose millions of dollars daily, since Israel's economy and life totally stop when she is mobilized for war. In 1956, and 1967, Israel chose the second course, the "preventive attack," winning territory and admiration from some quarters. But she acquired more internal problems and enmity from other nations.

In November 1967, the United Nations argued that the annexing of territory through conquest was inadmissible and resolved that permanent peace in the Middle East should be based on Israeli withdrawal to her pre-1967 boundaries, and on Arab recognition of Israel.

Jewish Immigration to Israel: 1948 - 1951 (total: 684,275)

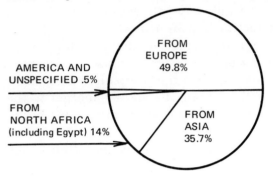

Israel Office of Information in "The Middle East — a Political and Economic Survey", Second Edition, 1954, p. 299.

Jewish Immigration to Israel:

	America, Europe, Oceana	Asia & Africa
1919 - 1948	89.6%	10.4%
1948 - 1966	45.5%	54.5%

Israel: Ministry of Foreign Affairs, Information Division, in *Facts About Israel, 1969,* p. 59.

World Jewish Population : 1971 : 13,951,000

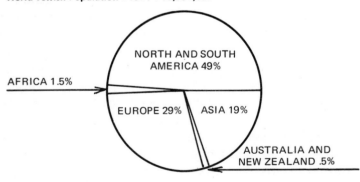

Source: *American Jewish Yearbook,* 1971

But an impasse developed. The Arab states will not recognize Israel until she has withdrawn, and Israel will not withdraw until the Arab nations recognize Israel within the terms of a permanent peace settlement.

Furthermore, neither the Arabs nor the Israelis have much confidence in the United Nations and its resolutions. Israel, particularly, has been shaken in recent years because many newly independent nations joining the United Nations have consistently voted against her. This "Third World" trend against Israel exists in spite of widespread assistance programs carried out by Israel in Africa and Asia. Some Black Moslems in America who have identified with "Third World" have caused many Black Americans and their sympathizers to favor the Palestinians. So crucial to the future of the Middle East is the Arab-Israeli conflict that our last chapter has been devoted to it.

JEWS OUTSIDE ISRAEL TODAY

The creation of Israel has had a tremendous influence on all Jews everywhere, regardless of their attitudes about Zionism. But Israel's greatest impact has been on Jews throughout the Middle East.

The Arabic-speaking Jews in countries from Morocco to Iraq have not been active participants in modern political Zionism. But the creation of the state of Israel forced these Arab Jews to make important decisions. For those who wanted to leave their Arab country of origin, several doors were open. Some went to Europe and America; most went to Israel. Still others, however, had little reason to leave. The modern Hebrew spoken in Israel was a foreign tongue to them; they had ancient family roots and favorable jobs and businesses where they were. The conclusion of the Austrian Herzl that Jews and non-Jews could not live together made little sense to them. Indeed, Jews had lived as minorities among non-Jews for many centuries in the Middle East with less tension than might have been expected.

Israel repeatedly voiced the claim that Jews everywhere belonged to her and sided with her policies. As tensions increased between Zionism and Arab nationalisms, therefore, Arabs began to question the loyalty of Jews in their countries. Was the first loyalty of Arab Jews to Egypt, or Iraq, or Syria, or whatever their nation happened to be? After 1948, tensions increased as Israel, by Zionism's definition, became the historic homeland to which all Jewish people were openly encouraged to return. With virtual war between the Arab nations and Israel going on since 1948, the condition of Jews in Arab countries has depended on how the Arab leaders have interpreted Israel's claims. Actually, most Middle Eastern Jews over the last twenty years have left their homes for Israel or other countries. Of 120 thousand Jews in Iraq in 1947, some tracing their families back to Babylonian captivity or to the family of Abraham, only about two thousand remain. Lebanon still has half its 1948 Jewish population of six thousand; Syria retains only four thousand out of thirty thousand in 1948; Egypt may have as few as twenty-five hundred out of the 120 thousand she had when Israel was created.

Israel is deeply concerned about the present condition of Jews everywhere, but especially in Arab countries. When Arab nations have called for a United Nations investigation of the condition of Arabs in territories occupied by Israel since 1967, the Israeli Government has refused and countered by insisting upon parallel investigations into the conditions of Jews in Arab countries.

No United Nations investigations have as yet taken place. As a matter of fact, today the status of Jews in many Arab cities depends to some degree on how strongly Arab leaders hold to their present conviction that Zionism is a minority movement supported by Western Jews but largely ignored by Jewish citizens of Arab nations.

When Israel withdrew in 1957 from the areas she occupied in the Suez war of 1956, she expected in return permanent recognition by the Arab states. But relations between Israel and her Arab neighbors have worsened, making Israel more conscious of her dependence on support from Jews around the world. Today Israel refuses to withdraw from the territories she occupied in 1967 without firmer guarantees than she had in 1956. Yet peace with her neighbors is Israel's highest priority for the future. How she will achieve it is a daily concern of her 2.5 million Jews. As deeply involved are the 11.5 million Jews elsewhere who, because of Israel's dilemma, have supported her and have become increasingly conscious of their own Jewishness. The prospects for this peace will be the subject of our final chapter.

QUESTIONS FOR DISCUSSION

1. What do political and religious leaders in your community think about the Middle East? Find out more about America's economic role in the Middle East.

2. Discuss differences between Judaism as a religion, Zionism as a world-wide political movement, and Israeli nationalism.

3. On what basis do some European and American Jews

oppose Zionism and Israel's policies although they support her right to be recognized as a state by the Arabs?

4. How would you have felt about the British and Arabs if you had been a refugee escaping Nazi Germany and settling in Palestine?

V. THE ARMENIANS:
A REVOLUTION THAT FAILED

The horse and the mule had a scramble and the donkey got trampled over.

An Armenian Proverb.

ORIGINS

Mount Ararat, midway between the Black and Caspian Seas, was for centuries the center of Armenia, a lofty symbol of the hopes of her people. Today it is the point of intersection of three nations—Turkey, Iran, and Russia. Only north of Mt. Ararat does today's map give us a hint of the past, for there is the Armenian Soviet Socialist Republic. Older members of her 2.5 million people remember well the last phases of a revolution that failed. The story of Armenia is the story of an ancient people invaded from north and south alike, caught in the struggles between East and West, and destined by history to be shared with many nations.

Oral tradition traces Armenian origins to Haic, son of Togarmah, the great-grandson of Noah. The ancient civilizations of Armenia are associated with the Hittites, Phrygians, and Babylonians. In the heart of Armenia,

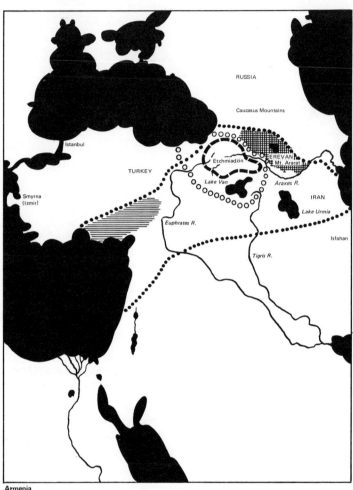

Armenia

●●●●●●●●●●● Armenian Empire under Tigranes (94-55 B.C.)

▤▤▤▤▤ Cilician Kingdom of Armenia
or Lesser Armenia (1080 - 1375)

▬▬▬▬▬▶ Republic of Armenia (1918-1920)

OOOOOOOO   Armenia by Treaty of Paris (Sèvres)
as drawn by President Wilson
for United States Mandate

▦▦▦▦ Present Armenian Socialist Republic in Russia

the foothills of the Pontus and Caucasus mountains, are the sources of the great Tigris and Euphrates rivers. Some have speculated that neither the Nile Valley nor Mesopotamia was the cradle of civilization, but that man's origins were in Armenia, the land of Ararat.

ARMENIA AS PART OF THE THIRD WORLD

While we can only speculate about her origins, one fact dominates this central area of the Fertile Crescent—Armenia's forests and steppes were constantly quarreled over by the two greater powers, Egypt and Mesopotamia. Armenia, like Syria-Palestine, has always been caught in a "Third World" position. Thanks to her mountains it has been more difficult for outside powers to control her people than it was for them to seize Syria-Palestine.

The Armenians appeared as a modern people when Cyrus the Great of Persia dominated the Middle East in the fifth century B.C. After Alexander's conquests in 323 B.C., the royal Armenian dynasty of Artzxias extended its power from the Caspian Sea to the borders of Egypt for a brief period under Tigranes (94-55 B.C.) until Roman armies ousted it. The Romans and Partho-Persians struggled for control of Armenia, which was on a major trade route between southern Europe and China.

Armenian tradition relates that the Apostles Thaddeus and Bartholomew brought Christianity to Armenia early in the first century. About 300 A.D., Gregory the Illuminator made Christianity Armenia's national faith —a dozen years before Constantine made it the religion of the Roman Empire. Often called "Gregorian" Christians, Armenians have always stressed that they were the first Christian nation in history. Unfortunately, in their enthusiasm for the new faith, they destroyed many pre-Christian temples, statues, and pieces of art.

The adoption of Christianity represented more than just a break with the past for two reasons. First, in choosing Christianity, the Armenians turned away from Zoroastrian Persia and later from the Muslim-dominated East and toward Christian Byzantium. Historical circumstances forced them to continue to look to Byzantium and later to Europe for survival.

Second, Christianity brought an internally divided Armenia together under a united spirit, bringing about a political, cultural, and religious awakening. In later years, however, the same church suffered from internal divisions. An important contribution of the Armenian renaissance of the fifth and sixth centuries, went beyond the rich heritage of Armenian art and literature itself. The Armenian alphabet, created in 404 A.D., enabled Armenian monks to translate into Armenian some Syriac, Greek, and other scholarly and religious works, the originals of which were subsequently destroyed in the many invasions of the period. We know of their existence today only through their Armenian versions.

This cultural renaissance in Armenia may have been the greatest sustainer of hope in a time of despair. As a result of the wars between the Byzantines and Persians, Armenia was divided between them in 387 A.D. In the Arab-Byzantine wars after 636 A.D., Armenia was again the combat zone. Like the Copts and Jews, the Armenians enjoyed more rights after the seventh century Arab Conquest than previously under the Byzantine Christians, who considered Armenian Christianity heretical.

Scattered Armenian settlements remained in several areas of the Byzantine Empire, but most Armenians stayed in their ancestral homeland. By the time of the military showdown between Byzantium and the Turks in 1071, Armenians found themselves fighting on both sides. After the Ottomans won, some Armenians went to south-central Turkey and founded a principality, which, with European support, grew into the Cilician Kingdom of Lesser Armenia (1080-1375).

ALLIANCES WITH OUTSIDE FORCES

In the Middle Ages, lesser Armenia provided arms, men, horses, and food for the Crusaders, a policy that later made Armenians suspect during times of outside threats. In the 1400s, the Venetians made trading treaties with the Armenians, at the expense of Syrian merchants. In 1514, after years of rivalry, the Ottoman Turks and Safavid Persians divided Armenia. Again a core of Armenians remained, but thousands migrated to other nations. Shah Abbas I of Persia (1585-1628) brought an industrious settlement of Armenians to Isfahan, to encourage by their presence trade and cultural ties with Western nations.

Settlements of Armenians from India to Europe became important in the struggle for Armenian independence. Their Gregorian Church, their language, and their culture remained links that bound together the destinies of Armenians in the historic homeland with the fate of Armenians in other nations.

The printing of books and pamphlets is always a part of any political awakening. A printing press was set up by Armenian exiles in Vienna, and the first book in Armenian was printed in 1512, just half a century after Gutenberg's invention of movable type. This Armenian press was moved to Constantinople in 1567, bringing more European ideas to the Armenian communities in the Ottoman Empire. Another Armenian press in a monastery in northern Persia was the first press in Iran. The Armenian community in Madras, India, published a book in 1773, in which there appears a reference to George Washington and his liberation movement against English colonialism. It was a call for Armenians in Turkey to write a constitution and demand independence from Turkey as Americans were doing in the New World.

Because of their scattered and very active communities in Europe and Asia, the Armenians were alert to world events. During the 1500s, Armenians in Persia and Turkey appealed to Europe for assistance against Turkish domination. One request went directly to the Pope, who, though he remembered Armenian aid during the Crusades, was not willing to help Armenians unless the Gregorian Church recognized Rome as the true church.

When Armenians heard that Peter the Great had become Tsar of Russia, they sent a request in 1716, telling of their hopes for Russian aid in delivering Armenia from the Muslim Turks. Tsar Peter was more eager to further his own purposes than to help the Armenians, but often both goals coincided. Appeals were made also to English dukes through Armenian communities in England. News of the French Revolution (1789) quickly reached Armenia, and when Napoleon invaded Egypt a decade later Armenians hoped that he would move up into Turkey and liberate them from the Ottomans.

ARMENIANS AND THE OTTOMAN EMPIRE

Why did Armenians hate their situation in Turkey? Perhaps they had forgotten by the eighteenth and nineteenth centuries how much worse life had been under the Byzantine Christians than under the Arabs and Ottomans. New ideas had filtered to them from Armenian students and church leaders abroad, building up their hopes for a return to the independent Armenia of the past.

Before the days of complete Ottoman control, the Armenians in central Turkey had worked out a system of survival with the numerous Kurdish mountain clansmen who were skilled fighters and cherished their own independence. The sedentary, agriculturalist Armenians gave a portion of their crops to specific Kurdish tribes in return for protection. This system worked so well that one Kurdish tribe would even fight another for "molesting our Armenians."

When the Ottomans made the Armenians a *millet* with their own spiritual head representing them in Istanbul, the urbanized Armenians saw this clergyman as a political figure rather than a national religious spokesman. For the Armenian villages in the interior, the *millet* system had little impact at all until the Ottoman Government began to enforce the collection of taxes. The Armenian villagers could not afford to pay tribute to both their Kurdish protectors *and* the Ottoman Government, but if they chose to pay the Kurds, the Ottoman soldiers enforced tax payment. If they chose the Ottomans, the Kurds attacked them. Like the Jews who were killed by both Crusader and Muslim, the Armenians were accused by both Ottomans and Kurds of being on the other's side. The Armenians for understandable reasons developed a persecution complex over the years which in turn became a cause of further persecution.

The Armenian dream of independence was nurtured by the interest of Western Powers, especially Russia, France, and England. This hope continued to be fortified by a second factor—Armenians abroad who were the chief living link between Armenians in Turkey and the Western Powers. Recognition of the Armenian *millet* within Turkey by Istanbul was the third factor that encouraged the Armenians to see themselves as a "nation" (the meaning of *millet* in Turkish).

But the *millet* system created its own divisions. It gave primary recognition to religious leadership at a time when a new generation of Armenians had a secular concept of national independence. The Armenian *millet* in Turkey was divided internally over religious and political questions. The problem was compounded in 1831, when Turkey recognized Catholic Armenians as a *millet* whose spiritual allegiance was to Rome, although Armenian Catholics were Ottoman citizens. By 1847, Protestant mission work (mostly American) had created a community large enough to be recognized by the Ottomans as a third separate Armenian *millet*. The Protestant schools were of special importance in bringing new ideas from the West, in nurturing nationalist sentiment, and in educating women. Three Armenian representatives in Istanbul instead of only one could have been used to their advantage. But dissension among the three *millets* (Gregorian, Roman Catholic, and Protestant) weakened the position the Armenians presented to the Western Powers in their attempt to obtain help in their struggle for liberation.

The Turks, remembering the days when Armenian troops helped the Ottomans expand their empire, claimed that the Armenians were a favored minority. Furthermore, Armenians were well educated and scattered over the Middle East as merchants and craftsmen. Because they spoke Turkish as their second language, many held important posts in Ottoman administrations in the Middle East. The Ottoman province of Egypt had a surprising number of Armenians in its government.

There is a paradox in the life of many minorities that is illustrated well in the Armenian case. On the whole, life under the Ottomans was good enough for Armenians to prosper, but that very prosperity created an envy among Turks and Arabs that turned into animosity against the Armenians as a people. For minorities, prosperity is never a substitute for liberty and security, or for the desire to be involved in the decisions that determine their future. Turks tended to prejudge Armenians as proud, pushy, and prosperous. Armenians, on the other hand, stereotyped the Turks as lazy and ignorant.

ARMENIAN NATIONALISM

The turning point in Armenian fortunes paralleled the rise of Russia and the hope every Tsar had of gaining access to the warm water ports of the Mediterranean Sea. Russia reawakened the Armenian hope that Western powers would help them win freedom. In the first thirty years of the nineteenth century, while Britain was still quarreling with her former American colony, Russia annexed the parts of Persia north of the Araxis River with encouragement from Armenians living in the area. Turkey was the real target of Russian ambitions, and periodic clashes were common in the 1800s. A war between Russia and Turkey in 1828, ended with Russia annexing sections of Armenia. In another fifty years the Russians had a more decisive war with Turkey, and the new "Armenian" Russians, as we shall see, played a major role politically and militarily.

Armenians under Russian sovereignty faced the same problem of self-identity as did their brothers in Turkey. Were they Russians first and Armenians second, or was their first loyalty to the "Armenian Fatherland"? Some, feeling that they were Russians of Armenian origin, put their stakes in Russia's future. Others saw themselves as Russia's Armenian "guests" whose life goal was to reestablish a free Armenia.

There was nothing unique about Armenian nationalism at this time, nor were Armenian hopes exaggerated in the context of the nineteenth century. Greek nationalists remembered the days of Alexander the Great. With English help, they wrested the Greek homeland from Turkey. Balkan groups under Ottoman rule were making similar historic claims and receiving aid from Europe in the name of religion, justice, and independence. The Zionists, harking back to the time of King David (900 B.C.), were making claims on Palestine. The Armenians were among dozens of peoples experiencing national and cultural revivals.

The next Russo-Turkish war ended rapidly in 1878 with striking Russian success. Many Russian soldiers were Armenians—a few were high-ranking officers. Furthermore, the Turks were convinced that Turkish Armenians had helped defeat Turkey from within. Life for the Armenian minority became increasingly difficult.

Important treaties in Cyprus and Berlin officially ended this war in 1878. Russia and England continued their own "cold war" over whose right it was to "protect the Armenians" in Turkey. By now the Armenians needed protection more than ever; but paradoxically the actions of the Great Powers on their behalf actually increased their insecurity. In short, Armenian nationalists tried to use the Great Powers to attain Armenian goals, while the Great Powers were exploiting Armenian nationalism to further their own ends.

This situation divided the Armenians even more. Few adopted the position the Copts took in Egypt —siding with the majority population (Turks) of their country against the powers of Europe. For Armenians the question was which European power to ally with. Some saw Russia as their best hope and pushed hard for all Armenians to put their efforts in Russo-Armenian cooperation. Others were oriented more toward England. A third faction wanted Italy and France as their "protectors." Divisions often took religious lines, the Gregorians favoring Russia; the Protestants, England; and the Catholics, Italy and France.

SEARCH FOR PEACEFUL SOLUTIONS

At the Congress of Berlin in 1878, the Europeans were primarily concerned with what they called the "Eastern Question"—that is, the role of Europe in dealing with the Ottoman Empire and its minorities. Sultan Abdul Hamid II believed the minorities to be well-off under the Ottoman *millet* system, and he viewed the whole problem of European intervention as "The Western Question." At Berlin the discussion focused on the Balkans. The Armenians were scarcely mentioned. Britain thought that all Armenians in Ottoman domains should be under her protection. But Russia, with traditional ties to Eastern Orthodoxy, believed she should informally protect the Gregorians. France assumed rights over the Roman Catholic Armenians.

The Armenian delegates to the Congress of Berlin had believed that the European Powers would convince Turkey to let Armenia be an autonomous state. They returned disappointed, bitter, and determined to take some kind of action. One of the delegates to the Congress was Archbishop Khirimian. His historic sermon at the Armenian cathedral in Istanbul, upon his return, was an indirect call to arms. He told how the Armenians had gone to Berlin armed with a petition. In the great council halls the European Powers placed on the table before them a "Dish of Liberty." In single file the Bulgarians, Serbians, and other Balkan nations passed by the table scooping out portions for themselves with "iron spoons." When the Armenian turn came, their "paper spoon" of petition crumbled, denying them even a taste.

TURN TO ARMED STRUGGLE

The Armenians concluded that the Europeans had greater respect for the armed revolutions of the Balkans than for Armenian petitions. Indeed, many of the Balkan nations did become independent from Turkey. After the failure of the Armenian petition at the Berlin Congress, many Armenians turned to "iron spoons" because their "paper spoons" had failed.

Several Armenian political societies emerged. Some were nationalist, some socialist, but all focused on setting up Armenian self-rule, even if it meant armed revolution. Of course these societies were secret. They sought aid more than ever from the West—especially from Russia. But by 1890, the Russians were as busy with the Siberian Railway and their Eastern frontier as America was with her Western frontier. Thus Britain remained Armenia's best hope.

Younger Armenians of all professions joined in the struggle. Some wanted to use violence, others preferred trying to work within the system. The Armenian churches took no official position but many individual ministers were active in the movement. In 1894, some two hundred thousand Armenians were killed by Turkish soldiers suppressing a revolt. News of this massacre was spread in Europe by friends of the Armenian liberation movements. Britain urged Turkey to reform its civil rights policies and considered intervening with troops. Russia and France restrained Britain, who did not want to act alone.

Truth is always the first casualty in times of crisis, and rumors were rampant. Many Turks believed stories that the Armenians, with European assistance, were planning to overthrow the Sultan. Sporadic massacres of Armenians continued throughout Turkey. The Armenian Catholics, under French protection, were spared, indicating that Turkish suspicions of Britain and Russia were the primary cause of these atrocities. Yet many Armenians were saved by Turkish Muslim friends. Nevertheless the Armenians believed that the Turks were preparing to kill them all. Britain, having taken Egypt from the Ottomans in 1882, cooled in her concern for the Armenians. Furthermore, her competition with France and Germany in the scramble for African colonies diverted her attention to her own empire.

The bitterness Armenians felt toward the West in general but toward England in particular was very deep. An Armenian poet relates the sacrifices of Armenian heroes thus:

Six centuries, drop by drop, the tyrant drains
The last remaining life blood from our veins;

Yet Europe says, No strength no power have they
And turns from us her scornful face away.

Some Armenian revolutionaries showed their anger
at Europe by seizing the Imperial Ottoman Bank in Istanbul, which represented millions of dollars in European investment. In the riots that followed, some seven
thousand more Armenians were killed. By 1896, about
four hundred thousand Armenians had perished out of
their total population of two million.

In the early 1900s the secret societies gained more
support for their belief that Armenia's hope rested in
freedom fighters alone. The struggle had reached the
point where some were willing to give their lives while
hundreds of others supported them indirectly. These
dedicated Armenian guerrillas were feared and re-
spected by the Turks and Kurds who called them
fedayeen. This was the Arabic name for "one who sacrifices himself," dating back to the "Assassins" of Crusader times (See Chapter III, p. 68). By the eve of World
War I, the Ottoman Empire was already crumbling, and
the Turks were faced with a guerrilla war within their
borders. Fearing that, as in the past, a Russian invasion in
1915, would be supported by Armenians in Turkey, the
Turkish government in one rash operation deported
nearly the entire Armenian population of Turkey, and
confiscated its property. Only Istanbul and two other
cities were untouched by this mass deportation. The
hardships of this deportation killed hundreds of
thousands. Some Armenian villages fought to the last
man as the Jewish defenders of Masada; a few were saved
by the advance of the Russian army. Most Armenians
were deported southward and those who survived expanded the small but ancient Armenian communities of

Syria, Lebanon, and Egypt. Many came to Europe and America.

RETURN TO THE CONFERENCE TABLES

But Armenians still had one hope. What they had lost at the Congress of Berlin and on the battlefield, they felt they would gain at the Paris Peace Conference after World War I. Some two hundred thousand Armenians fought on the Allied side even after thousands of their compatriots had been massacred. The self-determination championed by the American President Wilson spoke directly to their hopes. In the same treaty that in 1920, determined the post-war divisions of the Middle East, Armenian independence was recognized by Turkey and the Allies—but the treaty was never ratified. One alternate plan was for Armenia to become an American mandate, but the United States Senate rejected this in spite of President Wilson's recommendation. While the fate of Armenia was still being discussed, "iron spoons" once more decided the question as Turkish troops reconquered Turkish Armenia in December 1920.

During the First World War, the Communist Revolution had taken place in Russia. In 1921, Armenian areas not under Turkish control became part of a Transcaucasian Soviet Republic, and fifteen years later Soviet Armenia itself became one of the Soviet Socialist Republics. The Armenians in Turkey brought one more "paper spoon" to the Lausanne Conference of 1923, petitioning for a national home in Turkey. Again they were refused.

ARMENIANS TODAY

Today Armenians are of many opinions concerning

their past and future. In the Middle East there are few Armenians who would prefer emigrating to Russian Armenia. Some still talk occasionally of an independent Armenia and live as though in temporary exile. Wherever they live in large enough communities, many Armenians preserve their cultural traditions, close family ties, and some form of the Armenian church. Most Armenian family names end in "-ian" or "-yan" although those who prefer to become assimilated change their names to blend into the majority culture of their society.

Wherever Armenians have gone their rich cultural past has been remembered, and their skills have contributed to the development of their new country. William Saroyan, whose parents came from Armenia, has left his mark on American literature. Aram Khatchaturian is equally renowed in the world of music. Every part of society has seen contributions by Armenians.

A list of famous Armenians in Russia would be much longer. The best known to Americans is Anastas Mikoyan, who was President of the Soviet Union from 1964 to 1965. An aircraft designer of the same Mikoyan family joined the first two letters of his name to the first letter of his partner's name (Gurevich) to name their design of one of Russia's most successful airplanes—the MIG.

Why the Armenian revolution failed will be debated by historians and politicians as long as there are Armenians and other minorities caught in similar dilemmas. Among the most ancient people in the world, the Armenians have outlived many of their conquerors. In their twenty-five centuries of recorded history they have had only brief periods of independence. Although the Armenian people failed to attain permanent political autonomy,   their   greatest   successes   have   been lasting contributions to the civilizations of the past and to many nations in the modern world.

QUESTIONS FOR DISCUSSION

1. What does the historian Arnold Toynbee mean by saying that the Armenians are "the Jews of Turkey?" Why do you think the Armenians failed to establish an independent homeland, while the Zionists succeeded?

2. What do you think might have happened if the Armenians had joined the Turks in a common destiny as the Copts did with the Muslim majority in Egypt?

3. Do you know Americans of Armenian origin? Have the Armenians who have come to America assimilated into American society or do they live in their own communities preserving their own culture and religion?

4. Do you think America should have accepted Armenia as a mandate under the League of Nations after World War I?

5. How do you think the Armenian proverb about the horse, mule, and donkey (at the beginning of this chapter) relates to the Armenian experience?

Population of Palestine: 1918 — 1946

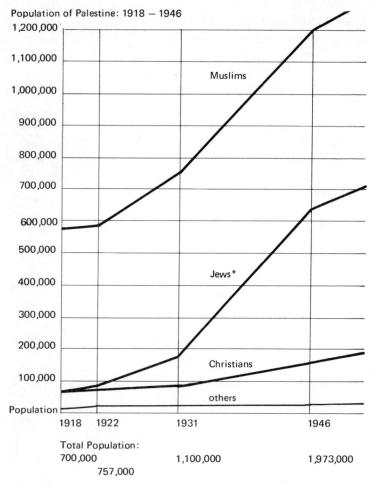

*Does not include Jewish immigrants who entered Palestine illegally according to British law.

Source: Government of Palestine: *Survey of Palestine,* Volume 1 and Statistical Abstract of Palestine, 1941.
Official Records of the United Nations Ad Hoc Committee on Palestine Question.
As in Henry Cattan, *Palestine, The Arabs and Israel,* p. 21.

VI. THE PALESTINIANS:
PEOPLE WITHOUT A COUNTRY

> *my will is hard like a rock*
> *and my fist is a tornado*
> *a fatalist, i am not*
> *my destiny i shape*
> *i'm one of the freedom fighters*
> *i'm one of them*
> *since i carried my gun*
> *Palestine is near*

From "the case" by Nizar Qabbani, Palestinian poet.

PALESTINIANS TODAY

None of the five groups we are studying has a definable religious, cultural, ethnic, and national identity. Copts, Jews, and Armenians existed as peoples before they became identified with the religions they later adopted. Although the Shias are a religious branch of Islam, religion plays no special role in the development of Palestinian nationalism, and Palestinians cannot be defined in ethnic terms. Although their origins go back to most of the conquerors who have settled in Syria-Palestine, the nationalistic concept of "Palestinianism" which unites them today goes back only to the time of the Paris Peace Conference (1919) when the former Palestinian province of Ottoman Syria was made a British mandate under the League of Nations.

Before the creation of Israel, "Palestinian" referred to all the indigenous peoples of Palestine—Muslims, Jews, Christians, and members of many other religious or cultural groups. Since 1948, as a result of the creation of Israel, Palestinians have been divided into several groups. The Palestinian Jews who remain in Israel today are part of the oriental Jews who form about 60 percent of Israel's Jewish population. The 150 thousand non-Jewish Palestinians who remained within Israeli borders after the 1948 war are referred to as Israel's Arab minority. Since the June 1967 war, about one million more Palestinians are in Israeli-occupied lands.

A third group of Palestinians since 1948 has been the refugees. In 1948, about eight hundred thousand were displaced, most settling in the United Nations camps in Jordan, Lebanon, Syria, and Egypt. A few migrated to Europe and the Americas. Especially after the June 1967 war, new faces have been added to the image of the Palestinian refugees—the Palestinian guerrilla —drafted from among the young men and women who have grown up in the bitterness and frustration of the refugee camps.

PALESTINIAN ORIGINS

The earliest inhabitants of the area once called Palestine were semi-nomadic tribes. The first people of record who actually settled on the coast and fertile plains were the Amorites and Canaanites. About 2000 B.C., they built towns and developed their own way of life.

The Hebrew Scriptures refer to this area as the "Land of Canaan." The Greek name for Canaan was Phoenicia. It was the geographical center of the Fertile Crescent, alternating between Egyptian and Mesopotamian influence. About the twelfth century B.C., Canaan/Phoenicia was invaded from the north by Philistines and from the south (Egypt) by Hebrews under Moses and Joshua. Joshua made a treaty with the Gibeonites (of Amorite origin) and co-existed with the Jebusites (Canaanites) who occupied Jerusalem (See Chapter IV). Although the Israelite conquest eliminated the majority of Canaanites, the Israelites were never able to displace the Philistines from the coastal area, probably due to the latter's use of more advanced iron weapons. The word Palestine comes from "Philistine," used by Greek and Latin writers in the first century A.D.

The Palestinians were not an ancient people in the sense that the Jews, Copts, and Armenians are. Most nations have been named after specific peoples, but Palestine became a geographical area that has probably been the home of more people over a longer period of time than any other place on earth. The ancient history of the Palestinians is the history of peoples of many faiths and cultures, caught between the ambitions of Egypt and Mesopotamia. Palestine has been a part of the "Third World" for four thousand years, often determining the balance of power between the ancient "superpowers" but becoming, nevertheless, the ultimate victim of their rivalry.

PALESTINE AND THE CHRISTIANS

In Chapter IV we surveyed the history of the Palestinian Jews up to the destruction of their Second Temple

by the Romans in 70 A.D. Until that time the history
of other religious and cultural groups in Palestine was
not much different. Indeed, Roman persecution of Jews
was soon followed by their persecution of Christians until
Christianity became the majority religion of the Empire.
Then Christian leaders in their new position of power
became persecutors.

From 300 to 600 A.D., Palestine became increasingly important to the Christianized Roman Empire. In Jerusalem, Emperor Constantine I had the
Church of the Holy Sepulchre built over the believed site
of Christ's tomb. His mother, Helena, had constructed
the Church of the Ascension and the Church of the
Nativity in Bethlehem. Palestine soon became a center
for Christian pilgrims who referred to Palestine as the
"Holy Land." Many monasteries flourished in the coun-
tryside surrounding Jerusalem. As noted in Chapter IV,
this Christian era was a difficult period for Jews
throughout the Byzantine Empire, but persecution was
worst in Palestine. Some Western pilgims settled in Palestine, adding even more cultural mixtures into the Palestinian crucible.

PALESTINE AND THE ARAB MUSLIMS

Islam came in 637 A.D., which, together with
the Arabic language, left a permanent heritage in Palestine, as in the rest of the Middle East. A predominantly
Christian Palestine became predominantly Muslim after
several generations, but Jewish, Christian, and other minorities remained. Under the Arabs, Christians continued to make pilgrimages to Palestine, and the restrictions
that the former Christian government had placed on
Jews were lifted. The Byzantines had surrendered

Jerusalem peacefully in 637 A.D., to Omar, the second Caliph. One of his first acts was to find the site of Solomon's temple which had been covered with earth since the Romans destroyed it in 70 A.D. Clearing the temple site, which was holy to Islam, he had a mosque built beside it. The Mosque of Omar is near the spot where Mohammed is said to have ascended briefly into heaven. In 691, the magnificent Dome of the Rock was built over the area. The fact that the sites of the ancient Jewish temple and the present Dome of the Rock (Mosque of Omar) overlap adds religious fervor to the present impasse between Israel and her neighbors.

By the time the Crusaders were calling for a liberation of the "Holy Land" from the Turks, Palestine had long been a holy land for all three faiths. The Arabic word for Jerusalem means "The Holy Place," and Muslims used to face Jerusalem when praying. As we noted in Chapter IV, the Crusades were a disaster for all the indigenous peoples of Palestine, especially the Jewish minority. Of course the East-West trade and communications that the Crusades encouraged had beneficial aspects. Many Crusaders intermarried with Palestinians and in the long run simply became another layer of people who intruded briefly into Palestine, dominated temporarily, and then melted into the population.

Even the Arab conquerors from the desert were absorbed into the ancient Palestinian population, but the Arabs were more than intruders. After 1,282 years (637-1919) of Islamic civilization in which all Palestinians (Jews, Christians, and Muslims) played an important role, Islam remained the dominant religion and Arabic the mother tongue of the area under the British until 1948. The Arabic language, more than any other cultural or religious factor, has made the descendents of the original inhabitants of Palestine identify themselves as Arabs.

PALESTINE AND THE OTTOMAN EMPIRE

Even four hundred years of Ottoman rule (1518-1917) did little to change the basic "Arabness" of the culture, language, and customs of the Palestinians. Christian Palestinians belonged to various *millets* under the Ottomans depending on their sect or rite; Palestinian Jews belonged to the Jewish *millet*; the Armenians, Assyrians, Druzes, and others belonged to their own *millets*. All spoke Arabic, and all had representatives in Istanbul. Palestine constituted three administrative units of the Syrian Province, whose capital was Damascus. These three units, Acre, Nablus, and Jerusalem, were like American counties. But Jerusalem, because of its special religious significance, was linked directly to Istanbul.

By the beginning of this century, Palestine was different from other Arabic-speaking areas of the Ottoman Empire in at least two respects. First, the degree of reverence that Jerusalem was accorded by Judaism, Christianity, and Islam was unique not only in the Ottoman Empire but in the entire world. Second, Palestinians of all faiths had reached a comparatively high level of political maturity and cultural achievement.

WORLD WAR I

It has been argued that people are ready for independence whenever they are politically mature enough to demand it. During World War I, the non-Turkish peoples of the Ottoman Empire wanted to be on their own. Judging by these standards and by their level of culture and education, we might say that the people of Palestine were better prepared to run their own country than were the people of any other Arab province of the Ottoman Empire. Yet, as we noted in Chapter I, the European Powers, especially Britain, France, and Russia, were more concerned with defeating Germany and Turkey than with fulfilling Arab hopes.

While General Allenby marched across North Africa into British-dominated Egypt, Arabs attacked the Turkish flank from Iraq and Saudi Arabia. The Allies made promises of Arab independence to Sharif Hussein of Mecca in particular and to "the inhabitants of territories occupied by Allied Armies" in general and that the future of these areas would be based on the consent of the governed after Turkey was defeated. Arabs from Syria, Lebanon, and Palestine rallied behind Sharif Hussein to support England, France, and Russia. Hussein was the great-grandfather of the present King Hussein of Jordan. His title Sharif indicated he belonged to the family (Hashemite) of the Prophet Mohammed (See Chart p. 64).

But Britain also wanted Jewish support for the war. The rise of Zionism and the Zionist goal of transforming Palestine into a Jewish homeland provided Lord Balfour with an opportunity to issue his declaration on behalf of Britain (See pp. 41, 42). The World Zionist Organization now had its first official positive response by a great power.

As we noted in Chapter I, Arabs and Zionist Jews outside Palestine felt deceived and bitter after the war, and those within Palestine doubly so. It has almost become a cliché to suggest that the problems of the "Promised Land" derive from its having been promised to too many people. But the end of World War I found Palestine once more occupied, this time by British troops, and indeed, the Palestinian Arabs were convinced that Britain would make Palestine an independent nation. The Zionists had equal reason to believe that Palestine was to become a Jewish homeland.

BETWEEN THE WORLD WARS

From this point on, the history of Palestine is one tragedy and misunderstanding after another. We have discussed the Zionist reaction to Britain (Chapter IV); what about the Palestinian Arabs?

The Jewish population of Palestine had increased at a normal rate from eight thousand in 1800 to twenty thousand in 1880. In 1918, the fifty-six thousand Jews were still less than 10 percent of the population of Palestine. With the increase in Zionist immigration after the First World War, Jews in Palestine numbered almost 11 percent in 1922. At first Palestinian Arabs were bitter only at Britain for what they felt was deception before and after the war. Many were open to the idea of more Jews coming to Palestine. As Jewish immigration accelerated under the British occupation of Palestine, however, some Palestinian Arabs began to feel that the Zionist objectives were part of a British colonial scheme to keep a foothold in the Middle East. Palestinian Arabs reminded Britain that the Balfour Declaration which favored a home in Palestine for Jews went on to say that "nothing should be done which may prejudice the civil and religious rights of existing non-Jewish communities in Palestine. . . ." Countries with Jewish minorities reminded Britain of the Declaration's final clause: ". . . .or the rights and political status enjoyed by the Jews in any other country." This was in reference to the Zionist claim to represent all Jews in the world and Zionist hopes of bringing all Jews to Palestine.

When Britain limited by law the immigration of Jews into Palestine, the Zionists saw this as a British-Arab attempt to undermine the purpose and goals of Zionism and the Balfour Declaration. Under Article 22 of the Convention of the League of Nations, Britain had promised that the "well-being and development" of the Palestinians formed "a sacred trust of civilization." Furthermore, the same article promised that the existence of the people of Palestine "as an independent nation was provisionally recognized."

As was clear to many statesmen at the time, the stage was being set for a confrontation. Palestinian Arabs were aware that the greatest support for the Zionist program came from Europe and North America. They learned that a report of the American King-Crane Commission to the Paris Peace Conference had to the contrary recommended "serious modification of the extreme Zionist Program for Palestine. . . ."

Palestinian Arabs on the whole had a Hollywood concept of America—a small British colony that had won its independence in a colonial war, expanded across western frontiers and was champion of the industrial revolution and international guardian of human rights. President Wilson's insistence that all peoples have "self-determination" gave the Palestinian Arabs confidence that their interpretation of justice would prevail. As late as 1948, they still represented more than two-thirds of Palestine's population and owned nine-tenths of the land. The Palestinian Arabs assumed that their wishes

Palestinian guerrillas practice the use of a Soviet made grenov anti aircraft gun south of the Sea of Galilee.

would prevail over the minority, many of whom were recent arrivals, who wanted to make the area into a Jewish state.

But the stage was set with blatant contradictions. The harder Britain tried to satisfy the contradictory hopes of both the Zionists and the Palestinian Arabs, the more intense their hatred grew for Britain and for each other. Following the Turkish example, Britain allowed some autonomy to the communities of Palestine. Thus the Jews had their local leadership as did the Muslims, Christians, and Druzes. Many differences within each community weakened their common opposition to Britain and to each other, but when it came to the question of Zionist immigration, the Muslim, Christian, and Druze communities united in protest. Divisions between Jews were likewise bridged by the threat of the Arab majority, although Palestinian Jews were not eager to create a Jewish state, and many opposed Zionist aims.

What was more alarming to the Palestinian Arabs than the percentage of increase in Jewish immigration was the fact that between the wars these Jews came primarily from European countries. Between 1922 and 1939, most Jews coming to Palestine were from Poland and Germany. These immigrants were well educated, maintained close relations with the Jewish communities in their countries of origin, and were quick to develop a modern economic, political, and social system for the Zionist community in Palestine. The more they came, the more Palestinian Arabs feared that Palestine was becoming a Europeanized Jewish state.

While the Zionists organized the Jewish community with increasing effectiveness, Palestinian Arab solidarity found expression only in times of special crisis, such as the anti-Zionist Arab revolt and the general strike of

1936-37. Britain arrested most of the leaders of this revolt. The remaining leaders fled from Palestine, leaving the Palestinian Arabs less organized than ever. But with the rise of Arab nationalisms, the surrounding countries considered the Zionists a threat to all Arabs. By 1939, Britain, which wanted to regain Arab confidence throughout the Middle East, and sympathized increasingly with Palestine's dilemma, allowed the other Arab countries to be spokesmen for the disorganized Palestinian Arabs.

THE NAZI AFTERMATH

By 1946, the Jewish population of Palestine had jumped to almost 33 percent. On January 27, 1944, the American Congress resolved that America use its good offices for Jewish "colonization, so that the Jewish people may ultimately reconstitute Palestine as a free and democratic Jewish commonwealth." Other Western nations joined in similar actions, calling on Britain to be more humane to the victims of Nazi racism. Britain, frustrated in the face of her impossible task, deposited the whole question at the door of the newly constituted United Nations.

The Arabs in general and the Palestinian Arabs in particular could hardly believe it when the United Nations Resolution of November 29, 1947, recommended that more than half of Palestine be assigned to less than a third of the population (most of whom were recent immigrants) who owned less than a tenth of the land. The Palestinians were not asked to vote in this decision about the future of their land. Palestinians believe that the 1947 United Nations Resolution succeeded because of last-minute American pressure that won the decisive votes of Nationalist China, Ethiopia, Haiti, Liberia, and the Philippines. The Palestinian Arabs recall that most of the Palestinian Jews (Arabic-speaking and mostly Orthodox) did not favor this partition. The United Nations Resolution ignited a series of violent protests in Palestine.

So serious were the events in Palestine after the partition resolution that the United States Government suggested reconsideration, even a possible temporary United Nations trusteeship over Palestine. But international political deliberations could not keep up with events in Palestine itself. The Palestinian Arabs were now convinced that the Zionists had the Western powers behind them, and that Britain, in withdrawing from Palestine, was selling her best weapons to the Zionist forces. A surprise massacre on April 9, 1948, by Zionist commandos, of unarmed Arab villagers in Deir Yassin just outside Jerusalem, was thought by the Palestinian Arabs to be deliberate and unprovoked. They point to this tragedy as the chief cause behind the Palestinian Arab exodus of 1948. Fear in the aftermath of Deir Yassin, the breakdown of security, and the chaos and anarchy following the departure of Britain increased the exodus of the disorganized Arabs. Thus some Palestinian Arab refugees fled previous to the Arab-Israeli war of May 1948, while others became refugees as a result of the war.

About eight hundred thousand Palestinians became refugees in 1948. More than half of them came from areas allocated to Palestine by the United Nations but conquered by Israel in the war. About 150 thousand Arab Palestinians remained in Israel. Most of the refugees poured into Trans-Jordan, which tripled its population and incorporated that part of Palestine not occupied by Israel. This included half of Jerusalem—the old city—containing the areas so sacred to Judaism, Christianity, and Islam. Now that the Hashemite Kingdom had land on both sides of the Jordan river it was called Jordan rather than Trans-Jordan.

PALESTINIAN EXODUS

But the conflict was only in its beginnings stages. The Palestinians vowed that they would return to Palestine, many refusing to leave the United Nations makeshift camps unless it was to return to their homes and farms now in Israel. They viewed any suggestion of permanent resettlement as a step away from their hope of return.

The first attempts at mediation and reconciliation evoked violent reactions from all sides. As early as September 1948, United Nations mediator, Count Bernadotte of Sweden was assassinated by Jewish guerrillas. The Palestine question seriously affected every neighboring Arab government. King Abdullah of Jordan, said to have secretly sought mediation with Israel, was assassinated in 1957, by a Palestinian refugee.

For almost twenty years the word Palestinian was synonymous with "refugees," people kept alive in camps by the United Nations on a budget of less than ten cents a day per person. Some Palestinians had relatives in other parts of the Middle East or elsewhere and sought new lives there. Some quickly rose to responsible positions in government and business in their new homes. Few, however, could forget the hatred and distrust that had surrounded the loss of their homes and farmlands in Palestine. In their new locations, Palestinians became increasingly skillful at explaining their position to the world.

POSITIONS AND POLARIZATIONS

For almost twenty years most Palestinians believed that by interpreting their position to the world quietly but effectively, they would someday be able to return to their former lands. They were convinced that the 1948 war was instigated by Zionist forces who wanted more land than was recommended by the United Nations partition of 1947. Some Palestinians refuse to recognize the validity of Zionist claims to any land at all in Palestine. The United Nations Resolution 194 (III) which was first passed on December 11, 1948, and has been reaffirmed every year since, recognizes the right of the Palestinian refugees to return to their homes. When Palestinians and other Arabs are told that the United Nations has no force with which to implement this resolution, they ask why United Nations Forces were used to enforce United Nations decisions in Korea (1950) and in Zaïre (the former Congo Kinshasa) (1960) but not in the Middle East.

To Palestinians, the wars in 1956 (Suez) and 1967 (Six-Day War) were a repeat of 1948. Many believe that Israel's hope is to restore the boundaries of the ancient Kingdom during the time of David; still other Palestinians are convinced that Israel will not stop until she has conquered the lands between the Nile and the Euphrates rivers. Israel's refusal to implement the United Nations Resolution of November 1967, is based on the Arab refusal to negotiate first; the Arab governments argue that the use of military occupation of lands gained by aggression to extract political gains will only justify further aggression (See Chapter VII).

The Palestinians ask their Western friends why Palestinian Arabs should pay for the anti-Jewish feelings of Europe by ceding their homes to the survivors of the

Nazi gas chambers. Palestinians point to the record of Jewish life under the Arabs not as ideal but as far superior to the anti-Jewish experience in the Christian West. To Palestinians, Zionism is a twentieth-century Jewish Crusade, originating out of anti-Judaism in Europe and seizing Middle Eastern lands by force.

NEW FACTORS

Twenty years of conflict have hardened both sides in different ways. Recent events suggest that the younger generation in Israel, especially those who are too young to remember the Nazi era, are doing some serious re-thinking about their relations with the Arab world. But it is still the older generation that holds power and is taking a tougher stand. On the other hand, the younger Palestinians who were born in refugee camps have become a tougher breed than their parents. Some *fedayeen* are as young as eleven years old. Bitterness and hatred are their only memories. Yet, ironically there is more hope of agreement between them and younger Israelis than between them and Arab governments, or the Soviet Union or the United States.

Palestinians are tired of talking and waiting for their concept of justice to be implemented by distant powers who seem to have forgotten Palestine. They are not trying to win favorable opinion in Europe and America. Nor do they see themselves as pro-Western or pro-communist. They are primarily pro-Palestinian. They are bitterly opposed to many Arab governments, especially the Arab monarchies.

While the present Palestinian commandos were still in primary school, Vietnamese peasants defeated French troops in Indochina (1954) and then successfully took on

America. Arab Algerians rose up against France using the same principle of a people's army made up of guerrillas backed by the majority of the population. Moreover, Palestinians think back to the Zionist-organized guerrilla war against Britain as the main reason why Israel was created so quickly and efficiently. Since 1967, the few Palestinians who were engaged in guerrilla warfare all along have been joined by growing numbers of idealistic youths who feel that history has taught them that arms gain more than diplomacy, especially for the weaker peoples of the "Third World." For Palestinians, the 1967 war was the turning point; until then they still held some hope that America would force Israel to comply with the United Nations. They have now turned to a war of liberation.

In short, the dispossessed Palestinians have increasingly identified with the peoples of the "Third World." Criticized for turning to arms, they have pointed out that twenty-three years of diplomatic efforts have failed. Criticized for their liberty-or-death, non-negotiable stand, they argue that they have nothing negotiable—no land, no rights, no power—to be recognized at the bargaining table. They are not recognized by Israel.

As in the past, the Palestinians are splintered politically into many factions. Even the most militant members of their guerrilla organization are divided on politics and strategy. Some favor hijacking planes, others concentrating on local confrontation with Israel. Some would look to Peking for aid, others to Moscow, others to Washington or any other source. The Palestine Liberation Organization is a federation of most of the *fedayeen* movements. Their goals are close to the declaration of Fatah, the largest branch of Palestinian commandos: the creation of a "New Palestine of tomorrow, a unified and democratic, non-sectarian Palestine in which Christian, Moslem, and Jew worship, work, and enjoy equal rights." Fatah looks to Lebanon as a model of how many religions can work together in one government.

In recent years the Palestinian liberation movements have made a special effort to identify with movements of liberation in Asia and Latin America, but their greatest effort has been directed southward into Africa. Their cooperation extends especially to armed Black African movements in southern Africa and in Portuguese-held territories (Mozambique, Angola, Guinea/Bissau). Palestinians have also expressed solidarity with several minority movements in America.

Whatever happens in the Middle East, any permanent peace must take the Palestinians into consideration. Up to the present no one has been able to speak for them, but the Palestinians themselves are seldom heard of except in the context of bombings and plane hijackings. Should Israel, Syria, Lebanon, Jordan, and Egypt decide tomorrow on a secure and permanently recognized boundary (which is very unlikely), the Palestinians would still have to be considered. In 1971, Jordan's army fought the Palestinian guerrilla movement in Jordan's major cities. So strong were the *fedayeen* that American troops stood by in the event that Hussein's army might be overpowered. Palestinian commando groups were greatly weakened by this civil war and have had to move to other Arab countries.

Will the Palestinian revolution be defeated as Armenia's was, or will parts of the areas presently occupied by Israel be made into a Palestinian state along the lines of the United Nations recommendation of 1947? Or will other solutions emerge? There can be no peace in the Middle East as long as enough Palestinians are convinced that armed struggle is less violent than the "violence" of a life without home, rights, or country—as long as there are those willing to "give up their lives," the *fedayeen*.

QUESTIONS FOR DISCUSSION

1. How would you answer the Palestinians who think that Israel should have been created out of Nazi lands in Germany after World War II instead of in the Middle East?

2. If you were a Palestinian Arab which position would you take? (Settle elsewhere, fight, work through the United Nations, others)

3. How would you describe America's role in the conflict between modern Zionism and Palestinian nationalism?

4. Why did the United Nations use force in Korea and in Zaïre (the Congo) to carry out its resolutions but not to enforce its resolutions on the Middle East?

5. Could you propose a peace settlement for the Middle East? Where would the Palestinians fit in?

VII. THE STRUGGLE BETWEEN MODERN ZIONISM AND PALESTINIAN NATIONALISM

Today's headlines on the Middle East usually focus on the war between Israel and her neighbors—a war that began before Palestine was divided and that has intensified year by year. No one can really understand the deep bitterness behind this conflict unless he is a Jew whose relatives perished in a Nazi gas chamber or a Palestinian who lost his home and farm lands in 1948. But if he is either of these, his involvement is so intensely personal that there is no room for discussion. Each is convinced of the justice of his position—that the land belongs to him. Each is willing to die for his cause.

To understand how people feel is more important than to argue whether their feelings are justified. Although we cannot completely understand the intensity of this long and bitter war, there are six basic points that are helpful as a base from which most of the issues can be discussed. These can help us understand how Palestinians and Israelis feel.

First, we must avoid the simplification that this is a war between "Jews and Arabs," with "The Jews" depicted as a boxer in one corner of the ring and "The Arabs" in the other corner. There is no single "Jewish" or "Arab" position. Of the fourteen million Jews in the world, only two and a half million live in Israel. As in any democracy, Israelis disagree about foreign policy. Some would seek peace immediately even if they have to let thousands of Palestinians return to their former lands. Others want Israel to remain primarily Jewish. Furthermore, there are some seventeen Arab countries whose major link is the Arabic language. They disagree widely over their policies toward Israel. To see "The Arabs" as a bloc of single-minded nations is false, although experiments in Pan-Arabism have been tried by small groups of Arab-speaking nations. We do not think of Spain and Peru as belonging to the same group of nations even though they are both Spanish-speaking. Similarly Lebanon and Sudan, for example, though both Arabic-speaking, are as different from each other as Spain is from Peru.

The seventeen Arab nations are not as crucial here as the nationless Palestinians, who are the crux of the problem. The conflict is not between Jews and Arabs but between modern Zionism and Palestinian nationalism. Both have many viewpoints, as we have seen. Both have allies. The major Arab states have championed the Palestinians since the beginning. Several Western nations have championed Zionist Israel.

The second point is the most misunderstood. The conflict is not a religious one although religious arguments have been used by all sides. The status of Jerusalem, for example, is a "religious" aspect of the greater problem which is basically a struggle of two peoples for the same land. All three faiths state that worship of God does not depend on a geographical place but on a special relationship between God and man. Jews in America and in other parts of the world are divided about Zionism; so are Christians and Muslims. Religion is an aspect of the

Palestinian-Zionist impasse only in the sense that religion is part of every aspect of Middle Eastern life. Furthermore, if this should develop into a religious war, the world will have returned to the politics of the Middle Ages. The Arabs would emphasize that there are more than twice as many Christians in Egypt and Lebanon as there are Jews in Israel, while the Muslims in the Middle East would organize their faithful throughout the world (half a billion in number) into a kind of Islamic "Zionist" movement.

The third point is obvious to anyone who reads newspapers or watches newscasts on television. Every act of violence in this war is in "retaliation" to a previous provocation by the other side. Thus we may hear one day of Israel's "retaliatory raid" against Palestinian *fedayeen* who bombed a bus the day before. The Arab newspapers report that this bus bombing was "retaliation" against Israel's leveling of Arab homes the day before that. What we must understand is that both sides are correct from their own understanding of history—from their own concept of their rights and destiny. If we trace the chain of retaliations back far enough, we find the Israelis reacting against thousands of years of Western hatred for Jews, epitomized by Hitler's Germany. We find the Palestinians retaliating against the sudden loss of everything they owned in 1948. During the 1972 Olympic Games in Munich, Germany, this cycle of violence reached a new peak when Palestinians kidnapped the Israeli team —most of whom died in a subsequent gun battle with German police. Israel then bombed several villages and commando bases in Syria and Lebanon. In early 1973, Israeli Terrorism and counter terrorism will remain until the root causes of this conflict are taken seriously by all sides.

Our fourth point underlines the frustrations of any hope for peace: every major argument in discussing the Zionist-Palestinian war has a counterargument equal in force and opposite in direction. Whether justified or not, the arguments, supported so intensely by each side, confront each other in hopeless deadlock. Israel does not recognize the existence of Palestinians; Palestinians do not recognize the existence of Israel.

Furthermore the Israelis are convinced that the Palestinians, backed by Egyptian, Syrian, Jordanian, and Iraqi armies, hope to push them into the sea; the Palestinians and their Arab neighbors are just as convinced that Israel's real aim is to expand Israel, pushing them into the desert. This is one reason why neighboring Arab states back the Palestinians, and why Israelis can depend on Jews everywhere to come to their aid even if they are not willing to come and live permanently in Israel.

After World War II, homeless Jews were used by Zionists to gain sympathy in the long process of establishing Israel as a state. Some plans to resettle Jews in the West after World War II were resisted by Zionists who feared that their success might defeat the possibility of creating a Jewish State in Palestine. Since 1948, many Palestinian refugees have also been used by Arab states. Their misery is displayed to gain support for the reestablishment of a Palestinian state. In both cases, however, many of the refugees suffered by choice because they believed in the righteousness of their cause.

The Palestinians, with no regular army or modern equipment, resort to terrorist tactics in a civilian population; the Jewish underground during the British Mandate over Palestine resorted to the same tactics for the same reasons. The arguments are endless, as are the counterarguments, but we must be familiar with them if we are to have any basic understanding of this conflict.

The fifth point is that most of the irreconcilable aspects of the Zionist-Palestinian war emerged from conference tables in Europe. Decisions were made in Europe about lands and peoples in the Middle East without considering the opinions of the people who owned the land. Permanent peace must depend on direct negotiations between Israel and all her Arab neighbors, especially the Palestinians, not on agreements between the Great Powers.

The sixth and final point deals with the way all sides view their present roles in the Middle East. The Arab states in general see themselves as part of the "Third World" and believe that Israel is part of the Western bloc's strategy for controlling them. Israel, on the other hand, believes she makes her own decisions. She is convinced that if the Arabs will come to peace terms, Israel's skills could be used to modernize the whole Middle East.

Many question marks punctuate the horizon, the greatest unknown being the role of the Great Powers. After 1967, the United States remained the only major supplier of arms to Israel, providing aircraft, missiles, and electronic systems in some cases of greater sophistication and strike capability than those provided to our NATO or SEATO allies. In 1971, the House of Representatives passed an amendment to the Defense Procurement Bill giving the President "open-ended" authority to transfer military equipment to Israel without limits on total cost.

While the United States has been providing arms to King Hussein of Jordan and other Arab monarchies, the Soviet Union has been increasing the flow of arms to Egypt. The reasoning of America and Russia sounds like the "retaliation" rationale of Israelis and Palestinians.

Washington declares that United States arms to Israel are to offset Soviet arms to Egypt, restoring a balance of power. Moscow replies that her defensive SAMS (Surface-to-Air Missiles) restore the balance upset by America's arms to Israel. The United Nations debates and discusses, but the countries in the Middle East continue to pursue their own policies. In any event, Israel remains a military and technological Goliath in the Middle East; the Arab countries are little Davids by comparison. But Israel's fear is realistic and understandable—a fear that her position may not always last.

The role of the People's Republic of China, with her many new interests in Africa and the Middle East is another unknown. China has always supported peoples' wars of liberation, and Chinese small arms have been used by Palestinian commandos for years. How will the replacement of Taiwan by China at the United Nations affect Middle Eastern politics and the Cold War? Shifting political winds in the post-Vietnam era promise changes of great importance. One of these changes will be the increasingly important role played by the Third World in international affairs.

Other developments, if they are to bring permanent settlement in the long dispute between modern Zionism and Palestinian nationalism, must respond in more realistic ways to the issues raised in the six points discussed above. It is very likely that the Zionist-Palestinian impasse will remain for some time the most divisive issue in the United Nations. The United Nations from the outside cannot hope to determine the future of the Middle East. Rather, we will be seeing events in the Middle East shape the United Nations agenda.

Finally, in this day and age anything written on the Zionist-Palestinian struggle is likely to be outdated almost before it is in print. However, whatever happens tomorrow in the Middle East will make sense only if we understand the past and present complexities of this tragic human dilemma. *the key to the solution.*

QUESTIONS FOR DISCUSSION

1. What other areas of the Third World were divided like Palestine after World War II? How have these been areas of dispute and warfare?

2. To what extent is the guerrilla war by Palestinians similar to other wars of national liberation in the world today?

3. What is American policy in the Zionist-Palestinian question?

CONCLUSION

By looking at only five minorities in the Middle East, we now have some concept of the complex problems of her nations today. The Middle East is the story of better-armed minorities conquering weaker peoples, being absorbed, and then in turn being conquered again. Each layer of civilization has left its impact on culture, language, and religion. Nationalisms have assumed many forms—most of them interwoven with religious concepts and born out of periods of cultural revival.

The impact of the West is still of major importance in the modern states of the Middle East. The advantages of technology and increased trade have been welcomed, but the breakdown of the Ottoman political order and old communal loyalties has left many new states competing for new loyalties at home and political partners abroad. New institutions, customs, standards, and laws have brought an insecurity that so often accompanies accelerated social change. Least affected by these changes have been language and religion.

In the face of these challenges, some minority communities like the Copts became assimilated, pledging primary loyalty to their new states rather than to their traditional cultural-religious community (*millet*). Others, like the Zionist Jews and Armenians, chose to seek autonomy even though it meant seeking outside help or resorting to guerrilla warfare. Some have sought support through their larger religious community—from fellow Muslims, Jews, or Christians in other parts of the world. Others have chosen to live in the kind of creative tension that we see in Lebanon, with a delicate balance of power among its many minorities. Minorities have played a decisive role in the cultural, economic, and political revolutions that have shaped the modern Middle East.

Some of the minorities in the Middle East, like the Copts, live in one compact area; others have areas of concentration with a broad scattering in distant cities and foreign lands: for example, Jews, Shias, and Armenians. Some, like the Palestinians, are widely scattered with no recognized center.

Above all, we have emphasized the common destiny of all minorities, especially those living in the Third World area between Egypt and Iraq (ancient Mesopotamia), caught historically in the crush between vying empire builders. Today the whole Middle East has become part of the larger Third World whose fate will depend on the role of the global super powers and the nature and direction of Middle Eastern nationalisms themselves.

SUGGESTED RESOURCE MATERIAL

CHAPTER I

Books

*Amin, Samir. *The Maghreb in the Modern World*. London: Penguin, 1970.

An Egyptian economics professor discusses the social and economic problems of Algeria, Tunisia, and Morocco with the conviction that their true political independence since French departure is impossible without economic independence.

*Cleveland, Ray. *The Middle East and South Asia*. Washington: Stryker-Post, rev. annually.

After brief chapters on the ancient empires and the rise and spread of Islam, there are short sections on each country today.

*Gendzier, Irene. *A Middle East Reader*. New York: Pegasus, 1969.

A collection of essays by Arab, Israeli, American, and British participants in recent events. Best on aspects of modernization.

*Goitein, S.D. *Jews and Arabs, Their Contacts Through the Ages*. New York: Schocken, 1964.

A penetrating exploration of three thousand years

of cultural, social, and intellectual contacts between two Semitic peoples.

*Hitti, Philip K. *The Arabs, A Short History*. Chicago: Henry Regnery, 1970.

A classic since its first publication in 1943. A leading Arab historian provides an introduction to their history and its meaning for the West. This is a briefer version of his *History of the Arabs*. Macmillan, 1956.

*Karpat, Kemal. *The Middle East and North Africa*. New York: Harcourt, 1968.

Emphasizes culture, peoples, and change especially during the Ottoman period. Special chapters on Israel and on the Middle East and North Africa in world affairs.

*Kirk, George E. *A Short History of the Middle East*. New York: Praeger, 1964.

A basic modern history from the rise of Islam to modern times. Excellent survey with basic facts.

*Lewis, Bernard. *The Arabs in History*. New York: Harper, 1960.

The most compact and concise account available of the Arab impact on history. Should be read with the author's more recent *The Middle East and the West*. New York: Harper, 1964, which describes the impact of the West on the Middle East.

Longrigg, Stephen H. *Oil in the Middle East*. New York: Oxford University Press, 1968.

First published in 1954, this is recognized as a standard work on the discovery and development of oil in the Middle East.

*Miller, David and Clark Moore, eds. *The Middle East Yesterday and Today*. New York: Bantam Pathfinder, 1970.

Selective series of short essays by experts on Middle East history. Begins at 600 A.D., ends with contemporary cultural, social, and economic issues.

*Peretz, Don. *The Middle East*. Boston: Houghton-Mifflin, 1969.

    Excellent treatment of history, peoples, cultures, religions, and contemporary problems. Good maps, illustrations, and charts.

Petrovich, M.B. and Philip Curtin. *The Human Achievement*. Morristown: Silver Burdett, 1967.

    Unit V treats the Islamic world in the context of world civilization. Excellent illustrations, art.

Scott, Sir Walter. *The Talisman*. Boston: Ginn, 1886.

    This classic novel about the Third Crusade (Richard the Lionhearted against Saladin) illustrates how many Western impressions of the Middle East have persisted over eight centuries.

Exhibits

A selection of photographs and paintings that can be borrowed for the cost of transport. American Friends of the Middle East, Inc. 1717 Massachusetts Ave. N.W., Washington, D.C. 20036.

Maps

Cultural map of the Middle East, double map supplement. *National Geographic,* Vol. 142, no. 1. July 1972.

CHAPTER II

Books

du Bourget, Pierre M. *The Art of the Copts.* New York: Crown, 1967.

    Beautifully illustrated and clearly explained by time periods up through the twelfth century. Fifty-six color plates, eighty-five figures.

Dick, Ignace. *What is the Christian Orient?* Westminster, Maryland: Newman Press, 1967.

>Explains in clear terms for Westerners the history and significance of Eastern Christian communities.

Hussein, Taha. *The Stream of Days*. New York: Longmans, 1948.

>A blind Egyptian scholar writes of his student days at Al Azhar University.

*James, T.G.H. *Egyptian Sculptures*. New York: Mentor, 1966.

>The Mentor-Unesco series. Excellent. Artistically illustrated with twenty-eight plates.

*Mansfield, Peter. *Nasser's Egypt*. Baltimore: Penguin African Library, 1969.

>An account of Egypt's entry into the twentieth century and the crucial role of the late President Gamal Abdel-Nasser.

*Rashid, Sidqi Bahijah, ed. *Egyptian Folk Songs*. New York: Oak, 1964.

>Traditional and modern, translated by the editor.

el Sadat, Anwar. *Revolt on the Nile*. New York: John Day, 1957.

>The successor of Abdel-Nasser relates his role in the revolution against King Farouk in 1952, eighteen years before he himself became President of Egypt.

*Stevens, Georgiana, G. *Egypt Yesterday and Today*. New York: Holt, 1963.

>A panoramic view of Egypt's post-revolution decade (1952-1962) set against the background of Egypt from ancient times. Good discussion of modern issues.

CHAPTER III

Books

Arberry, Arthur J. *The Koran Interpreted*. 3 vols. New York: Macmillan, 1955.

One of the best translations of the Koran into English, with index. Another English traslation is Mohammed M. Pickthall's *The Meaning of the Glorious Koran*. New York: Mentor, 1953. Also with index.

*Cragg, Kenneth. *The Call of the Minaret.* New York: Oxford, 1964.

A distinguished scholar of Islam explains its meaning in contemporary language.

*Esslemont, J.E. *Baha'u'llah and the New Era.* Wilmette, Illinois: Baha'i Publishing Trust, 1970.

First published in 1923, this is a good introduction to the Baha'i faith and its history from a sympathetic viewpoint.

*Hitti, Philip. *Makers of Arab History.* New York: Harper, 1971.

An introduction to religious, political, and cultural movements in Arab history through the lives of representative leaders.

Longrigg, Stephen and Frank Stoakes. *Iraq.* New York: Praeger, 1959.

Nations of the Modern World Series. A history of Iraq, her people, religion, and politics from early times through the revolution of July 1958.

Najafi, Najmeh. *A Wall and Three Willows.* New York: Harper, 1967.

Life in modern Iran as told to Helen Hinckley, whom the author knew while a student in America. The same authors have also written *Persia is My Heart*, 1953, and *Reveille for a Persian Village*, 1958.

Payne, Pierre S. Robert. *The Splendor of Persia.* New York: Knopf, 1957.

Persian greatness—her people, poetry, and art are paraded before the reader in simple style. Little on modern Iran.

Shah, Sir Mohammed (The Aga Khan). *The Memoirs of Aga Khan.* New York: Simon & Schuster, 1954.

His Highness the Aga Khan II(1877-1957) recalls

his life as the spiritual leader of Ismaili Islam from his boyhood in India to the League of Nations and World War II. Preface by his friend Somerset Maugham.

*Smith, Wilfred Cantwell. *Islam in Modern History*. Princeton: Princeton University Press, 1957.

A recognized scholar describes Islam and what is happening in the Muslim community today.

Stewart, Desmond. *Orphan with a Hoop. The Life of Emile Bustani*. London: Chapman and Hall, 1967.

A boy grows up near Sidon during the end of Turkish domination (World War I) becoming a Lebanese statesman and a well-known figure in the Arab World. A good view of the Arab world from within.

*Tor, Andrae. *Mohammed, The Man and His Faith*. New York: Harper Torchbacks, 1960.

First published in 1936, this remains the best introductory book on Mohammed and his impact on Islam.

*Ullah, Najib. *Islamic Literature: An Introductory History with Selections*. New York: Washington Square Press, 1963.

Selected readings (translated into English) of Arabic, Persian, and Turkish literature from pre-Islamic to modern times. Includes poetry, religion, science, and philosophy.

CHAPTER IV

Books

Berger, Elmer. *A Partisan History of Judaism*. New York: Devin-Adair, 1951.

An American rabbi, long outspoken against modern Zionism, believes that Jews are truer to their historic faith when they identify themselves with the country of their citizenship.

Chouraqui, Andre. *A History of Judaism*. New York: Walker, 1962.

A concise introduction to four millenia of Jewish history in clear and simple style.

Fine, M. and M. Himmelfarb, eds. *American Jewish Yearbook*. New York: American Jewish Committee and Jewish Publication Society of America. Published annually, this volume contains facts and articles about world Judaism. The 1968 edition has an article about Jews in Arab countries since the June 1967 War.

*Goldin, Judah, ed. *The Living Talmud*. New Haven: Yale University Press, 1955.

The wisdom and traditions of the great Hebrew sages of the past, selected and translated with an essay by the author.

*Heschel, Abraham Joshua. *Israel: An Echo of Eternity*. New York: Farrar, Straus, and Giroux, 1969.

One of America's most eminent rabbis speaks as an eloquent defender of Israel, stressing her spiritual significance for Jews and Judaism.

*Kitzinger, Ernest, *Israeli Mosaics of the Byzantine Period*. New York: Mentor, 1965.

The Mentor-Unesco series is beautifully illustrated with twenty-eight plates.

*Mintz, Ruth, ed. *Modern Hebrew Poetry: A Bilingual Anthology*. Berkeley: University of California Press, 1968.

A reprint of a 1966 edition with translation into English.

Saint John, Robert. *Ben-Gurion, A Biography*. Garden City: Doubleday, 1971.

A well-written story of the Russian-born Zionist pioneer who led the war of independence against Britain and became Israel's first prime minister in 1948.

Watson, Sally. *To Build a Land*. New York: Holt, 1957.
> Account of two Jewish war orphans who go to Israel and join in the struggle first against Britain, then against the Arab armies.

CHAPTER V

Books

Blatter, Dorothy. *Cap and Candle*. Philadelphia: Westminster, 1961.
> A Turkish girl dreams of becoming a nurse, but her family disagrees. Shows a dilemma of modern youth in traditional society.

Der Nersessian, Sirarpie. *Armenia and the Byzantine Empire*. Cambridge: Cambridge University Press, 1945.
> On Armenian art.

—————. *The Armenians*. New York: Praeger, 1970.
> Excellent on early history, society, economics, religion, literature, and art. Little on the modern period. Contains seventy-eight photos and forty-eight line drawings.

Gidney, James B. *A Mandate for Armenia*. Kent: Kent State University Press, 1967.
> Within the framework of Armenia's past and present, the author discusses the debate after World War I over the possibility of Armenia becoming an American mandate.

Housepian, Marjorie. *A Houseful of Love*. New York: Random House, 1957.
> Born of Armenian parents in New York, the author offers a most enjoyable novel about an Armenian family in America.

Kinross, Lord. *Attaturk, The Rebirth of a Nation*. London: Morrow, 1964.
> The story of the Ottoman Empire, World War I,

and the rebirth of Turkey as a republic under Ataturk (Mustafa Kemal). Mature Students.

*Lewis, Bernard. *The Emergence of Modern Turkey*. New York:
Oxford, 1968.
Comprehensive and thorough. Roles in history,
politics, economics, and religion in modern Turkey.

*Werfel, Franz. *The Forty Days of Musa Dagh*. New York: Pocket
Books, 1962.
A novel of World War I and the persecution of
Armenians in Musa Dagh (near ancient Antioch).

Yale, William. *The Near East*. Ann Arbor: University of
Michigan Press, 1968.
A modern history with proper emphasis given to
the Ottoman period and modern Turkey. Chapters on every country, on cultural and national
movements, and on social change.

CHAPTER VI

Books

Abu-Lughod, Ibrahim, ed. *The Transformation of Palestine*.
Evanston: Northwestern University Press, 1971.
A collection of essays by scholars (mostly Western)
treating several timely aspects of the creation of
Israel out of Palestine and explaining the positions
of the Palestinians.

*Aruri, Nasser and Edmund Ghareeg, eds. *Enemy of the Sun*.
Washington: 1970.
Poems of Palestinian resistance translated from
Arabic by the editors. Artistic sketchings. This book
notes how the poetry of these twelve Palestinians
bears a remarkable resemblance to the poetry of
Black America.

Cattan, Henry. *Palestine, The Arabs and Israel*. London: Long-mans, 1969.

    A Palestinian lawyer, presently practicing international law in England, presents a clear Palestinian perspective from personal experience. The author has a sequel which summarizes the above and updates events through the 1970 civil war in Jordan. *Palestine, The Road to Peace*. London: Longmans, 1971.

Furlongs, Geoffrey. *Palestine is My Country*. London: Murray, 1969.

    The story of a Palestinian Arab lawyer who lost his home in 1948.

Khadduri, Majdia, ed. *The Arab-Israeli Impasse*. Washington: Luce, 1968.

    A collection of essays by eminent international authorities who explain the Palestinian and other Arab positions. Some of the specialists are Arnold Toynbee, Albert Hourani, Jean Lecouture, Rabbi E. Berger, and former U.S. Ambassador to the UN., Charles Yost.

Stevens, Richard. *American Zionism and United States Foreign Policy*. New York: Pageant, 1962.

    An American scholar explores American Zionist support for Israel and its effect on American foreign policy.

GENERAL BIBLIOGRAPHY

*American Friends Service Committee, *Search for Peace in the Middle East*. Philadelphia: A.F.S.C., 1960 and Fawcett, 1970.

    A study of the Israeli-Palestinian question prepared in cooperation with Canadian and international Quaker groups. Nothing could better prepare readers for the intensity of this conflict than reading the above in conjunction with a reaction to it by the American Jewish Congress and the Anti-Defamation League of B'nai B'rith. **Truth and Peace in the Middle East, A Critical Analysis of the Quaker Report.* 1971.

Avneri, Uri. *Israel Without Zionists.* New York: Macmillan, 1968.

    A maverick member of Israel's parliament pleads for peace, concluding that it can come only by replacing Zionism with a secular and pluralistic ideology.

*Khouri, Fred. J. *The Arab-Israeli Dilemma.* Syracuse: Syracuse University Press, 1968.

    A scholarly, historical criticism and analysis of the policies of the Arab states, Israel, Russia, and the United States.

*Laqueur, Walter, ed. *The Israel-Arab Reader.* New York: Bantam, 1970.

    A collection of the most crucial historical documents by a widely recognized scholar of Middle Eastern Affairs.

Peretz, Don. *Israel and the Palestinian Arabs*. Washington: Middle East Institute, 1958.

A well-known American historian of the Middle East deals with the basic issues of the conflict. The author was in Palestine at the time of the 1948 war.

*Rodinson, Maxime. *Israel and the Arabs*. London: Penguin, 1968.

A French professor of oriental languages (Sorbonne) with long personal experience in the Middle East shows the contradictions of all sides and the ignorance and partiality of the West.

Taylor, Alan and Richard Tetlie, eds. *Palestine, A Search for Truth*. Washington: Public Affairs Press, 1971.

Twenty-one old and new scholars offer their approaches to the Israeli-Palestinian conflict.

Books

*Antonius, George. *The Arab Awakening*. New York: Putnam, 1965.

Classic work on the rise of Arab nationalism. First published in 1939.

Arberry, A.J., general ed. *Religion in the Middle East: Three Religions in Concord and Conflict*. 2 Vols. Cambridge: Cambridge University Press, 1969.

The first volume covers Christianity and Judaism. The second focuses on Islam. Many scholars contribute.

*Badeau, John S. *The American Approach to the Arab World*. New York: Harper, 1968.

Former U.S. Ambassador to the United Arab Republic and present director of the Middle East Institute at Columbia University, the author appeals for a realistic American policy.

*Brand, Charles M. *Icon and Minaret: Sources of Byzantine and Islamic Civilization*. Englewood Cliffs: Prentice Hall, 1969.

Insight into Byzantine and Islamic religion and culture from the fourth to fifteenth centuries.

*Chan, W.T. and others. *The Great Asian Religions*. New York: Macmillan, 1969.

Islam placed in the context of other great Asian religions. Anthology, extensive bibliography.

*Davidson, Roderic H. *Turkey*. Englewood Cliffs: Prentice Hall, 1968.

Scholarly, succinct treatment of Turkey as a modern nation.

Johnson-Davies, D., ed. *Modern Arab Short Stories*. London: Oxford, 1967.

A British writer selects and translates contemporary stories from the Arab world.

*Kritzic, James. *Anthology of Islamic Literature from the Rise of Islam to Modern Times*. New York: Mentor, 1965.

Includes drama, poetry, prose, proverbs, and scriptures up to 1800.

*Lenczowski, George, ed. *United States Interests in The Middle East*. American Enterprise Institute for Public Policy Research, 1968.

Political, economic, cultural, and historical survey of the deterioration of American relations with the Middle East.

*McNeill, William H. *The Rise of the West: A History of the Human Community*. New York: Mentor, 1965.

Excellent synthesis and history of the Western impact on the Third World.

Meyers, Bernard S. ed. *The McGraw-Hill Dictionary of Art*. New York:McGraw Hill, 1969.

Entries under peoples, cultures, and periods with an art bibliography for each entry. Many plates and illustrations.

Exhibits

Middle East Exhibits, 1761 N Street, Washington, D.C. 20036.
Has traveling exhibits (art, fashion, designs) available for the cost of transportation.

Bibliographies

American Friends of the Middle East, 1717 Massachusetts
Avenue N. W., Washington, D.C. 20036.
*1) *Basic Bibliography on the Middle East and North
Africa.*
*2) *Catalogue: Specialized Lending Library on the Middle East*, 82 pages. Covers every aspect of Middle
Eastern life.
American Historical Association, Service Center for Teachers of
History, 400 A Street S.E., Washington, D.C.
20003.
*1) Roderic H. Davison's bibliographical essay on
the *Near and Middle East* (Publication No. 24) is
excellent up to 1959. 48 pages.
*2) Margaret Faissler's annotated bibliography on
history books for pre-college readers (Publication
No. 1 is more updated (1965) containing ten pages
on ancient history and two pages on the Muslim
world).
Catholic Near East Welfare Association, 330 Madison Avenue,
New York, N. Y., 10017.
*1) *A Selected Bibliography on the Middle East for
Teachers and Students*, 16 pages, 25 cents. Books,
bibliographies, study guides.
*2) *Sources of Free and Inexpensive Materials on the
Near and Middle East*, 16 pages. Updated: film
sources, records, study guides, government publications, maps, posters, charts, bibliogaphies, and
organizations.

Howard, Harry and Edith Ehrman, eds. *The Middle East and North Africa.* Willamsport: Bro-Dart, 1971. 80 pages.

> Convenient and extensive bibliography by countries and subjects. Primarily for undergraduate libraries. Gives references for reviews of books listed.

Islamic Book Service, P.O. Box 3244, Milwaukee, Wisconsin, 53208.

> Provides lists of books and publications on Islam, as does Medina University Press International, 908 Ashland Ave., Wilmette, Illinois 60091.

Israel Information Services, 11 East 70th Street, New York, N.Y. 10021. *Selected books on Israel, 1969*, 15 pages.

> Historical, general, international relations, education, kibbutz, archaeology, religion, biography, literature, holocaust, cookbooks, and other areas.

Institute for Palestine Studies, Ashqar Building, Clemenceau Street, Beirut, Lebanon.

> Bibliography deals with the Palestine question.

Middle East Institute, 1761 N Street N.W., Washington, D.C. 20036.

> *1) "The Middle East in Paperback, II" by Harry Howard is a reprint of an excellent annotated bibliography from the *Middle East Journal*, Summer, 1969, 28 pages.
> *2) *The Middle East: A Selected Bibliography of Recent Works,* 1960-1970, 67 pages ($1.00).

Organizations and Information Centers

> The following organizations, listed alphabetically, represent a wide variety of attitudes and ideologies concerning the Middle East. Most have a bulletin or newsletter. The teacher and student may want to contact the following:

American-Arab Association for Commerce and Industry, 505 Fifth Avenue, New York, New York 10017.

American Friends of the Middle East, Inc., 1717 Massachusetts Avenue, N.W. Washington, D.C. 20036.

American Jewish Alternatives to Zionism, Inc. 133 E. 73rd Street, New York, N.Y. 10021.

American Jewish Committee, 165 East 56th Street, New York, N.Y. 10022.

American Zionist Youth Foundation, Inc., 515 Park Avenue, New York, N.Y. 10022.

Americans for Justice in the Middle East, Box 4841, Beirut, Lebanon.

Americans for Middle East Understanding, Inc., Room 538, 475 Riverside Drive, New York, N.Y. 10027. The November/December issue of *THE LINK* (1972) is devoted to resources on the Middle East.

Anti-Defamation League of B'nai B'rith, 315 Lexington Avenue, New York, N.Y. 10016.

Arab Information Center, 405 Lexington Avenue, New York, N.Y. 10017.

Association of Arab-American University Graduates, Inc., P.O. Box 85, North Dartmouth, Massachusetts 02747.

Catholic Near East Welfare Association, 330 Madison Avenue, New York, N.Y. 10017.

Committee on New Alternatives in the Middle East, 339 Lafayette Street, New York, N.Y. 10012.

Institute for Palestine Studies, Ashqar Building, Clemenceau Street, Beirut, Lebanon.

Israel: Information Division, Ministry of Foreign Affairs, Jerusalem, Israel.

Israel Information Service, 11 East 70th Street, New York, N.Y. 10021.

Jewish Peace Fellowship, 339 Lafayette Street, New York, New York 10012.

Middle East Institute, 1761 N Street N.W., Washington, D.C. 20036.

Middle East Research and Information Project, Box 3122 Columbia Heights Station, Washington, D.C. 20010.

Palestine Liberation Organization, 101 Park Avenue, Room 311, New York, N.Y. 10017.

Search for Justice and Equality in Palestine, P.O. Box 53, Waverly Mass. 02179

United Nations Public Information Office, United Nations, New York, N.Y. 10017.

Teaching Guides and Atlases

*Kenworthy, Leonard S. *Studying the Middle East in Elementary and Secondary Schools.* World Affairs Guides, New York: Teachers' College Press, 1968.

Overview, curriculum proposals, major concepts to stress, basic facts, activities and methods, resources and films (general and by country), addresses of organizations, publishers, and filmstrip companies.

*Kingsbury, Robert C. and Norman Pounds. *An Atlas of Middle Eastern Affairs.* New York: Praeger, 1964.

Maps with text of regions, empires, nations, and resources up to 1964. Excellent complement to Penguin Atlas below since it concentrates on the modern period.

*McEvedy, Colin. *The Penguin Atlas of Ancient History.* Baltimore: Penguin, 1970.

An artistic compilation of color maps and texts —beginning at 50,000 B.C. with Neanderthal man and depicting graphically the evolution of agriculture, races, languages, metallurgy, empires, towns, and trade up to 362 A.D.

Sharabi, H.B. *A Handbook on the Middle East.* Washington: Georgetown University Press, 1956.

Treats each section of the Middle East with introductory remarks followed by an annotated bibliography of books, articles, and periodicals.

*Williams, William A. *America and the Middle East: Open Door Imperialism or Englightened Leadership*. New York: Rinehart, 1958.
>Source: Problems in World Civilization Series.

Directories, Encyclopedias

Encyclopedia of Islam. 4 Vols. M.Th Houtsma, T. W. Arnold, R. Basset, and R. Hartman, eds. International Association of the Academies, London, Luzac, 1913.
>Leading orientalists cover the geography, ethnography, and biography of Islamic peoples. A one-volume, shorter *Encyclopedia of Islam* was published by Luzac in 1953. In 1960, a new edition of the 1913 series was begun but only the first two volumes (A through G) are completed.

Europa Publications Limited. *The Middle East and North Africa, 1970-'71*. London, 7th edition.
>A survey and directory of all countries. Concise information on every aspect. Includes a Who's Who.

Universal Jewish Encyclopedia. 10 Vols., Isaac Landman, ed. New York: Universal Jewish Encyclopedia, Inc., 1939.
>An authoritative popular presentation of Jews and Judaism since earliest times. Illustrated. Doubleday has a one-volume *New Standard Jewish Encyclopedia*. Drs. C. Roth and G. Wigoder eds. 1970.

Records

The following have catalogues listing records of folk and religious music of the Middle East:

Folkways/Scholastic Records, 906 Sylvan Avenue, Englewood Cliffs, New Jersey 07632.

Icon and Book Service, 2546 Belmont Avenue, Bronx, New York 10458.

Miro-Music Inc., P.O. Box 342, Old Chelsea Station, New
York, N.Y. 10011.

Audio-Visual

Most embassies (see last section of resource bibliography) have
films available on their country. An *Audio-Visual
Directory* is also available for $2.50 from Motion
Picture Enterprises, Inc. Tarrytown, New York
10591 listing sources nationwide and statewide.
For other films, filmstrips, and film listings see the
following:
Alba House Communications, Canfield, Ohio 44406. Film-
strips and records on Islam.
Alden Films, 5113 16th Avenue, Brooklyn, New York 11204.
Films of Israel. Listing also available from Israel
Information Services, 11 East 70th Street, N.Y.,
N.Y. 10021.
Anti-Defamation League of B'nai B'rith, 315 Lexington Av-
enue, New York, New York 10022. Films, film-
strips, and recordings on Jews, Judaism, and Israel.
Catalogue available.
Bowmar, Inc. 622 Rodier Drive, Glendale, California 91201.
Sound filmstrips with history and folk songs of
Israel and the Arab world.
Coronet Films, 65 East South Water Street, Chicago, Illinois
60601. Film catalogue avaiable.
Encyclopedia Britannica Educational Corporation, 425 North
Michigan avenue, Chicago, Illinois 60611. Film-
strips on ancient and modern periods.
International Communications Films, School and Library Di-
vision, Garden City Long Island, New York 11530.
Catalogue of films, filmstrips, and multimedia kits.
Life Educational Program, Box 834, Radio City Post Office,
New York, New York 10019. Filmstrip catalogue.
McGraw-Hill Films, Test-Film Division, 327 West 41st Street,

New York, N.Y. 10036. Catalogue: Series on Middle East.
Universal Education and Visual Arts, 221 Park Avenue South, New York, N.Y. 10003. Catalogue available.

Embassies

Algerian Interests Section, Embassy of the Republic of Guinea, 2118 Kalorama Road, N.W., Washington, D.C. 20008.
Embassy of Iran, 3005 Massachusetts Avenue, N.W., Washington, D.C. 20009.
Embassy of Israel, 1621 22nd Street, N.W., Washington, D.C. 20009.
Embassy of the Hashemite Kingdom of Jordan, 2319 Wyoming Avenue, N.W. Washington, D.C. 20008.
Embassy of the State of Kuwait, 2940 Tilden Street, N.W., Washington, D.C. 20008.
Embassy of Lebanon, 2560 28th Street, N.W., Washington, D.C. 20008.
Embassy of Libya, 2344 Massachusetts Avenue, N.W., Washington, D.C. 20008.
Embassy of Morocco, 1601 21st Street, N.W., Washington, D.C. 20009.
Embassy of Saudi Arabia, 1520 18th Street, N.W. Washington, D.C. 20036.
Embassy of Tunisia, 2408 Massachusetts Avenue, N.W., Washington, D.C. 20008.
Embassy of the Republic of Turkey, 2523 Massachusetts Avenue, N.W., Washington, D.C. 20008.
Iraqi Interests Section, Embassy of India, 1801 P Street, N.W., Washington, D.C. 20036.
United Arab Republic Interests Section, Embassy of India, 1801 P Street, N.W. Washington, D.C. 20036.
Yemeni Interests Section, Embassy of Somali Republic, 3421 Massachusetts Avenue, N.W., Washington, D.C. 20007.

INDEX